Shadow Chaser

Sean Austin
with David Weatherly

Enjoy!
Dorinda.

love.

Shadow Chaser

by Sean Austin with David Weatherly

ISBN: 978-1-945950-08-7 (Paperback)

Published by:

Leprechaun Productions
Nevada

Cover by: Sam Shearon
www.mister-sam.com

Editor: Dale Triplett
@DaleTriplett

Layout: SMAK
www.smakgraphics.com

Printed in the United States of America

Acknowledgements

It's my belief, that before we even land on the physical plane, our life's path is charted for us along with a list of things we are meant to accomplish. There are certain souls we are meant to come in contact with along our personal spiritual journeys on Earth. Every person that comes into your life is there for a specific reason and I want to give special thanks here to some of the individuals who have been important to me on my journey into the paranormal and the culmination of this book.

I want to thank my father and mother for the life they gave me. The beginning of my life, all the good and bad, helped shape me into the man I've become. My faith and my spiritual core are due in large part to my family's influence and it's helped keep me strong and protected.

Thanks to Ralph Sarchie for the experiences and the knowledge he's imparted to me. Ralph taught me to have a deep respect for "the work" and showed me the importance of servitude to God's will. He's a model of a man strong in faith and service to God. Bless you Ralph.

Thanks to fellow investigator Dave Spinks for his input and for taking me to some amazing locations during my journey. We've had some great times together and I look forward to many more crazy experiences on the paranormal road.

Thanks to investigator/author David Weatherly for his hard work on this book. I really appreciate his vast knowledge across the spectrum of the paranormal and all the locations we've investigated. I also want to thank him for publishing this book through his company Leprechaun Productions.

Thanks to artist Sam Shearon for the amazing cover art. Sam is an amazing and talented artist and brought my vision to life.

Thanks to Kimberly Carper for her sketches of the entities included in the book. Capturing the images of some of the creepy things I've encountered was no easy task, but Kimberly hit the mark.

Although I never met him in person, I have always felt a connection to Ed Warren and as you will read, he had an influence on me over the years. His books were some of the first paranormal books I read and had a big effect on me.

I'd also like to thank John Zaffis, another person with a vast amount of experience who I've learned a lot from over my time in the field.

Most of all, I want to thank God for the amazing experiences I've had so far in my life, and for all to come as I move forward on this amazing, spiritual journey.

Thanks to everyone else not mentioned by name who have been a part of my time in the paranormal.

Table of Contents

CHAPTER ONE:
My Beginnings

Six years ago, I couldn't see my future. I never could have guessed my journey would lead me to where I am today, writing a book about my paranormal experiences.

But I have come to understand the bizarre tales on the paranormal I had seen on television and read about in books are not just stories—they are real— and my personal brushes with the paranormal have changed my life forever in profound ways.

My outlook on life has changed. I long to make a difference and I hope something positive will result from my actions. God has given us all gifts and the use of them, to me, is life's grandest purpose.

My childhood was normal by most standards. I was raised in a Catholic family. I attended Catholic schools and church every Sunday. I was an altar boy.

Many people go through the motions when attending church and they pray to God out of childhood routine. Sometimes I did that too, however, other times I looked up towards the sky and felt I was having an authentic conversation with God. I prayed for things to come to fruition in my life and I prayed for guidance for whatever hurdles I was facing at the time. My thoughts would always turn to the possibility that my experience was real, the experience of communing with God.

Looking back, I can now identify omens in my life that lead me to where I am now. I believe these omens predicted my life's path and my spiritual future.

My mother said that as a child, I would tell strange stories about being in space and about memories of being in the womb. Strange fodder for a little boy to discuss.

Happy times with my family.

As I grew, there were other odd things I experienced. I remember the first incident. I was a young boy and I was at my family's beach house on Long Island, NY, just outside Westhampton Beach and close to the bay. It was right around the block from my maternal grandmother's house.

The house was on a long road that lead to a dead end at the bay. I ran up and down that street playing with the local children from the neighborhood. I have vivid memories of running through high, wheat-like grass between the homes on my way back to our house.

One time, out of the corner of my eye, I saw a book on the

ground. Curious as to what someone might have abandoned, I picked it up. Upon examination, it was some sort of Satanic book that had pages torn out and burned edges.

Frightened and almost in tears, I threw the book to the ground and ran as fast as I could back home. I shared the story of my scary find with my parents.

This experience has stood out in my mind and, looking back on my early life, my spirituality and my involvement in the paranormal, I feel that it had a great impact on my path.

From my early days, music has always been another important part of my life.

In 1991, Pearl Jam released their song "Jeremy." I'll never forget watching the music video for the first time. The song is about a teenager named Jeremy, a young man from a broken family. Isolated and with no love or affection from his parents, the poor kid decided to shoot himself in front of his high school class.

The song reflected a serious situation that is all too real in our modern world. Pearl Jam's lead singer, Eddie Vedder, had such a strange look in his eyes as he performed the song. It was as if he was possessed.

Emotions engulfed me as I watched the suicide myself. I felt as if I was Jeremy going through those dark events and feelings as things raced towards the last day of his tragic life. It was the first time I had chills while listening to a song. It reached down into my soul and triggered a response within me.

From that core feeling, my passion for writing, singing and playing music took a firm hold. I bought a guitar and took lessons for about three weeks before quitting. Not to abandon music, rather to teach myself so I could learn at a faster pace. I taught myself to play guitar, bass and drums. On my first solo CD, I played all the instruments myself.

I believe a good ear for creating and playing music is one of the gifts God gave me. From the time I wrote my first song, and had my first band, it all felt as natural as breathing. For years, my devotion to music flourished. I played with many different musicians throughout high school and well into my twenties. It was both a blessing and a learning process.

I was experiencing growth and personal success in music, but other aspects of life were more challenging. I believe, if you don't have an understanding of life from a spiritual standpoint, things can really mess with your head. Obstacles arose, and I wondered why I had to endure such challenges. Perhaps it was the inconvenience of immaturity and ignorance, but I understand now it was a necessary part of my growth.

By my mid-twenties, my family was going through some rough patches. My father had a successful temp agency that had given us a prosperous life, enabling us to have a beach home on Long Island, as well as other material blessings. I felt, and still feel, incredibly fortunate to have those childhood experiences ingrained in my memories. The beach house in particular gave me a sense of comfort and a deep appreciation of the ocean that remains with me to this day.

Unfortunately, my father's company was sabotaged by employee embezzlement. He didn't know the source of the lost money, and although the company stayed afloat for a while with tax money, he soon had to sell the business. Soon after the family fell apart.

Mom moved away, going to Florida, while my father, sister and I all stayed in New York. It was a humbling experience to say the least, and it took a toll on me. I sought solace by drinking heavily, trying to chase away the emotional fallout and aftermath of a broken family.

We all make mistakes. If we're fortunate, we (hopefully) learn from the mistakes and don't repeat them. Ultimately, we can come out much stronger on the other side of bad times.

Amid all these changes and challenges, I saw my childhood home of twenty-five years lost.

Still more bumps in the road came. I was trying to pursue a career in music and while doing so, I was managing a local Bronxville wine store. Probably not the best choice for someone challenged by alcohol, but God always has a plan.

People left me behind at the most vital moments in my pursuit for representation as a performing artist. I distanced myself from these people, while continuing to write songs expressing the trials and emotions I was going through at the time.

I needed to release my music. The songs were in my blood. I absolutely believe that music and spirituality go hand in hand, and despite the challenges the pursuit of music was probably one of my saving graces during this difficult period of my life.

Just by listening to a piece of music, emotions can be triggered within part of the soul, amplifying the feelings and sometimes purifying us or leading us to deeper understandings.

When it comes to discovering your passion, I believe it should be something that resonates so strongly that you would travel to the ends of the Earth to make it a central part of your life.

God gives each of us special gifts and we have the chance to make a difference with them in this physical plane of existence.

Whether we choose to go down that road and take the risks that come along with the pursuit of our passion is up to us. God granted us all free will when he created us.

There is a myriad of situations that can be presented, tragedies to endure, and challenges to face. We can cope, or not, in many ways. There are diverse methods that can bring brightness to our souls. Again, this lies within the spectrum of free will, our choice to do the right—or wrong—thing.

Whether you're brought up in a religious family, or don't follow any religion at all, I believe being a good person, and loving others the way you want to be loved yourself, is the essence of being human.

Reaching out to brighten the darkness in another's world is what God wants us to do. It makes us more like God, which I believe is the goal for our souls in our time here. This is something that transcends all belief systems. Having nothing but unconditional love and forgiveness for each other.

Although I was brought up Catholic, I now consider

myself Catholic/Spiritual as I've attempted to truly embrace God's lessons beyond the confines of the church's doctrine. For instance, I don't believe we all learn all the lessons we need for our souls to progress in a single lifetime. For this reason, I believe in reincarnation.

This doesn't change my core faith system. Instead I believe it broadens the depth of it and my beliefs. I truly believe we are all capable of reaching the heights of God's ultimate plan for us.

Knowing what I know now, I don't believe there is any concept of time in the spirit realm. Past, present and future are all one. We have a life chart before we are born; an overall plan of action for our soul with a chance to brighten our lives by taking a step closer to our soul mission.

I cherish the fact that I'm able to now look back at the hurdles I went through, and I have a deeper understanding of why it was happening. Not everyone is so fortunate, and I'm thankful for the opportunity to share my experiences in the hope of making a difference in other people's lives.

I went through several bad experiences in my music career and was screwed over on many occasions. It's a rough business and can be very harsh at times. I found myself in difficult circumstances and needed to make some money to finance my dreams and pay the bills. I had spent and lost thousands of dollars to shysters who failed to keep their promises.

Time is a scary thing you know? Complacency can be a seductive trap. A continual routine without progress feels like a hamster on a wheel, moving but not really going anywhere. It's tough to break unproductive routines. Sometimes even after seeing results you can start to feel guilty if you stray from your standard routine. You have to fight to make it to the top of the mountain and to attain the reality of the dream you hold within yourself.

It's difficult to depend on other people to help you obtain your goals, but it's part of the human experience.

While God offers guidance, it's critical that you believe in yourself.

Fear, I have found, is the food of demons.

CHAPTER ONE: My Beginnings

CHAPTER TWO:
The Paranormal Calls

When I started getting involved with the paranormal, the many strange experiences I'd had growing up started to make sense. While growing to adulthood and pursuing music, my spiritual abilities had awakened.

We're all born with natural psychic abilities, but we lose touch with them after being hammered with "rational" thoughts and the reality of the material world.

Spirits gravitate towards children because the young are fresh from the spirit realm themselves and not contaminated by the material world.

Some people try when they're young to talk to their parents about the things they experience; ghosts and imaginary friends, hearing deceased loved ones, in this children are very open. But most parents assure their kids that such things are not real, that there are no such things as spirits and the deceased are far removed. Hence, it's all imagination and best to ignore it, relax and go to sleep.

Some children have stronger natural gifts than others and it's not as easy to displace their abilities. If you have a child who has an imaginary friend, or is seeing something strange, pay close attention, they may be speaking the truth. Acknowledgement is a key element when it comes to spirit energy. It's vital to be careful and aware during these events. Acknowledgement, while important to children, can also attract and energize spirits, both positive and negative ones. Giving attention and energy to the wrong spirits potentially places you, your child, and your family in a dangerous spiritual situation.

Becoming a paranormal investigator is usually triggered by an experience or event in one's life. In my mid to late twenties, I found myself fascinated by the paranormal. I started watching documentaries and television shows about ghosts and hauntings.

As a child I had loved horror novels and movies. Ironically my first birthday fell on a Friday the 13th! By the fourth grade I was reading Stephen King books. Most horror films I found laughable—except one. The one film that gave me nightmares. "The Exorcist."

The movie was based on a novel by William Peter Blatty. Blatty was from Bronxville, the place I grew up and had spent most of my life.

Blatty's book was based on a series of real events involving the possession of a young boy. The story changed certain elements, including the gender of the possessed child.

One of the men featured in the story, a Jesuit priest, was one of the teachers at my high school, Fordham Prep.

Perhaps these connections caused the movie to hit home for me on a deeper level, affecting me at my core.

Like many genuine cases involving the demonic, the Exorcist story began with the use of a Ouija board.

In my experience, 95% of the cases of demonic infestation begin with the use of a Ouija board. A lot of people assume it's the actual board itself that is dangerous, but this isn't correct. It's the intent to energize an inanimate object to open a doorway to the spiritual realm that's dangerous. Giving permission to an invisible entity to move through you and use your body in an act of supernatural puppeteering is an extreme danger, and I believe it can lead to possession.

In the very process of trying to communicate with spirits,

an invitation is issued, and unseen entities can take advantage of the opening. They will then wreak havoc in any way they can. I consider toying with a Ouija board a spiritual version of Russian roulette.

Of course, possession and bad experiences don't happen every single time a board is used. Someone might play with it once or a hundred times and have nothing happen to them, but during any given session, a negative spirit could enter the situation. Is it really worth the risk?

Since there is no concept of time in the spirit realm, there is also the possibility that the effect of working with a Ouija board could manifest at any time in your life. Months or even years later a spirit you connected with through a board could decide to start interfering in your life. In these cases, the victim has often forgotten their time spent toying with the Ouija board, and may not even realize the root of their problem is paranormal in nature.

Author Sean Austin with the world's most haunted doll, Annabelle.

Anyone fascinated and passionate about being involved in the paranormal must understand that it's imperative to learn how to protect yourself. Walking into this realm by choice allows entities to come into your life. It's what I call "the spiritual rules of engagement."

If you choose to actively investigate haunted locations, it's important to understand you are voluntarily partaking in the energies attached to the location, and there is often risk involved. Going into such a situation one runs the risk of negative attacks, or of being followed by negative entities.

I don't believe God permits spirits or negative entities to come into our lives unless some kind of invitation has been issued. In a sense, the very act of going into an investigation creates an invitation to whatever is at the location, so caution and spiritual protection are a must.

At some time or other, we all walk into the unknown not knowing what could happen and what we may confront. It's dangerous and delicate to learn for beginners, but it's important to develop an understanding of how suddenly situations can erupt with malevolent energy. There can be physical aspects, objects moving, items being thrown, having your body touched, pushed or scratched, but these are the lesser concerns. We're least prepared for the psychological and spiritual attacks that can occur.

Demonic forces can sit dormant and wait patiently for an opportunity to attack, catching you off guard when you're least expecting it, months, even years later. A demon is a fallen angel and by nature, they are at war with human beings.

Lucifer was once the most beautiful of angels, but he rebelled against God with an army of his followers. This led to their downfall and their transformation into demons here on Earth. Lucifer and his followers didn't want to acknowledge God's creation of man.

Our souls came into our physical bodies with no prior knowledge of our origins or why we are here. That's part of what makes our lessons so important and special. With free will we can choose right or wrong.

Being consumed with power, greed and all the seven deadly sins is why Lucifer and his followers fought with God over the creation of humans.

Now, hiding in the shadows of our world, he and his minions wait for us to allow him to enter our lives and make an example out of us. This is accomplished by trying to influence us to hurt ourselves and others, and to show God in every way possible that he was mistaken in creating us.

Realizing this fact and understanding that a species we cannot physically see is at war with us illustrates how dangerous paranormal situations can be.

When I began to experiment with the paranormal for the first time, I read books about demonic hauntings and the paranormal in general to get a foundation in my mind. I wanted to know what the most extreme cases were like, and what the worse potentials were. I did this before I got involved as an investigator and I always strongly recommend others do the same before taking the big step. Education is key!

CHAPTER THREE:

Jenny

In my early thirties, I went out one night to a local cemetery purported to be haunted. The experience would turn out to be the beginning of transformative changes and would alter my outlook on life.

My friend Greg decided to join me at the cemetery that night. I had tried to get him to join me on previous occasions, but he never would. Greg is one of the biggest skeptics I've ever known. He would always laugh when I brought up the paranormal. I had grown close to Greg and even confided in him that I believed ghosts were real, still, there was no changing his personal belief.

The cemetery is an old one in Yonkers with graves dating back to the 1800's. People in the area had reported that not just one, but three "ladies in white" were chasing them out of the cemetery.

As we went up the hill into the graveyard, we found the first set of markers. They were all children's graves, always a sobering sight.

I decided to record some audio to see if we could capture any voices. I stopped at a small grave belonging to a girl named Jenny. Some of the markers had pictures on the graves, a kind and special thing to do for loved ones. I turned on the recorder and asked:

"Jenny are you still here?"

I was using my cell phone to record, and I held it close, waiting. I was certain I heard a voice come through my phone's speaker when I asked the question.

I stopped the recording but didn't listen to it, figuring I would check the recordings later. Greg and I walked through more of the cemetery. He joked and told me it was silly to "believe in this stuff." Nevertheless, I pursued my mission and asked some more questions at different points around the graveyard. Nothing extraordinary happened while we where there, and no women in white manifested to chase us away.

The next night back in my apartment, I sat down and played back the recordings I had made during our little adventure in the cemetery. The first one was my recording at Jenny's grave.

By my memory of the dates on the grave's marker, Jenny must have been about eight years old when she passed away. I listened to the recording and heard my own voice asking her if she was still here.

I almost went into shock from what I heard. It was undeniably the voice of a child responding to my question! It sounded like she responded with the statement:

"Two toys died."

It was an odd thing to say, that toys had died, but in a child's world, a broken toy can have a lot of impact. The EVP certainly had an impact on me. I had chills, I was a bit terrified, and at the same time I was exhilarated.

Excited and energized, I listened to the other recordings I made that night. I heard another voice speak the word "muerto," Spanish for death. In another recording, I asked if anyone would like to talk to the gentleman with me who didn't believe in ghosts.

Just then, I head a woman inhale, as if she was in shock. This was *my* moment. The moment when I knew—really knew—and realized, ghosts are real. My defining moment that confirmed so much for me personally.

In some ways it was a simple start perhaps. But hearing the voice of a spirit like that, a voice from someone who wasn't physically present, it was stunning.

EVPs (electronic voice phenomenon), like the ones I captured are the voices of disembodied spirits speaking from beyond the physical plane. Typically, spirits speak on a frequency that can't be heard by the human ear in real time. Investigators use recorders to capture such voices and sounds. The recordings pick up frequencies we can't normally hear.

I understand when skeptics question paranormal audio and video evidence. First hand experience is the optimum way to experience the paranormal, otherwise one could quickly discount the phenomena.

It's important to be objective about personal experiences. It's an easy trap to fall into the idea that everything is paranormal. It's critical to look at how events fit together, the synchronicities and collected data and information. Is the evidence from your equipment confirming your personal experience? Does the location exhibit tell-tale indicators of a haunted location?

It's a lot to consider, but once you develop your own rhythm and style of investigating you find a workable formula that works on a personal level.

All of these things and more were rushing through my mind as I listened again to the amazing EVPs from the cemetery. But on the level of personal experience, there was much, much more to come.

Two weeks after the trip to the cemetery, I woke up to see the shadow of a little girl at the right side of my bed. Caught by surprise, I yelled out in fear and threw my hands out. She disappeared. Now, I know what you may be thinking. That I was dreaming or that I was in that state of half sleep, but I wasn't. I know what I saw, and it was the clearly defined shadow of this little girl beside my bed.

Coupled with my first EVP recording of a little girl's voice, it was all clear to me. I was no longer watching paranormal shows and documentaries from a viewer's perspective. I was now there, on the front lines having first hand experiences.

During this time of my life, I was still managing the wine store. A lovely revolving door in my life that went on for ten years. Another friend came on to work at the store and we discovered we both had a common interest in the paranormal. Ironically, his name was also Greg.

Now there was the first Greg, the "skeptic" and my new friend who I call Gregory.

I told Gregory about my experience in the cemetery and the response from Jenny. Eager to get more EVP's, I headed off again, this time with Gregory the believer accompanying me.

This time I wanted to try to get direct responses to specific questions. Standing in front of a row of soldier's graves, I directed my question to the one in front of me and asked:

"Are you here with us?"

The response on the recorder was:

"I'm a different soldier."

We also returned to Jenny's grave. This time the recording yielded the voice of a little girl singing a song.

Honestly, it was creepy.

I'm sure many people wonder why God allows the spirits of children to be stuck. Although I can only speculate, I do have some theories.

I believe the tragedy of children dying sets off emotional waves through the loved ones who lose the child and it gives them the chance to learn and endure. To cope. Life isn't about being perfect, and learning is sometimes done through struggling. I'm not sure why it happens, but I believe the events of some deaths set up a variety of scenarios on the next plane of existence. I'm not sure that anything could make the loss of a child any easier, but I do believe such events are part of God's plan, as difficult as that can be.

Why are spirits stuck between worlds? Again, we can only speculate. Perhaps they have just not been able to find peace.

I believe the recipe for a ghost is a person attached to their location or another person. Sometimes they require justice for their death. Other's don't know they are dead. They may be consumed with guilt or realize the need to be accountable for their deeds in life. Maybe they are afraid to cross over. Such questions are always in my mind when I investigate haunted locations.

CHAPTER FOUR:

The Murder/Suicide House

Sometimes even the most terrifying moments are a gift from God and a means to learn more about your soul's mission. In the beginning of my investigative journey, I would often reflect on incidents and ask myself if it all really happened. Of course, I always came back to the fact that my experiences were real, they were just beyond what many people commonly accept as reality.

In a way, the paranormal field reminds me of the movie "The Matrix." There's a choice between the blue pill or the red pill, and once your moment to choose comes, there's really no turning back. At a certain point, it becomes a vital part of your life and you simply can't deny it or ignore it, because it will continue to peek its head into your world.

The lesson of the need to be constantly prepared on a mental, physical and spiritual level hit home when I investigated a house with an infamous and tragic story.

Decades ago, a husband bludgeoned his wife to death in their home. The couple's youngest daughter was across the hall when the murder occurred, and all indications are that she witnessed the event.

It was New Year's Eve. The woman had survived the attack but was barely alive. She was rushed to the hospital but died a week later, succumbing to the severe wounds inflicted on her in the brutal assault.

As all of this was unfolding, police were searching for the husband. It turned out he was indeed the murderer, but before he was captured he took his own life by jumping off a nearby bridge.

As if the horrific tale wasn't tragic enough, there was more. Years later, when one of the woman's daughters reached the same age as her stepfather was when he committed suicide at the bridge, the woman also took her own life—by jumping off the same bridge.

The daughter left a simple note behind on which she wrote: "Mom, I'm coming to look for you."

Perhaps she was tormented all those years by the tragedy that destroyed her family. It's difficult to imagine being haunted by such events and the toll they can take on the mind and spirit of a human being.

The house where the murder took place was on the route I took to and from work. Considering there were three tragic deaths associated with the home, I often thought about the possibility that some of the spirits were still there, restless and disturbed in the afterlife.

I finally told Gregory we should stop by the house one evening to see if we could capture any EVPs.

On our first visit to the house, we didn't even get out of the car. Parked in front of the home, I turned on my recorder and we began asking questions.

"Is the daughter still here?"

"Are any spirits residing here?"

Replaying the recording, we discovered that we had indeed captured a response. A female voice responded:

"Killed my mother is what killed me too."

We took a moment and let the unsettling response sink in before attempting more questions. Starting another session, we asked:

"Do the mother and daughter still live here?"

The recorded response this time was a female voice issuing a shrieking scream and the words *"Help me."* The plea was repeated several times. It was a hair-raising recording.

Still sitting in the car, we also asked about the murderer:

"Is the stepfather still here?"

Again, a response was captured on our recorder:

"I'm still here."

The recorded voice was so clear, it gave me a chill. It was as if the spirit of this man, this murderer, was sitting there in the car with us!

We'd had enough for the evening and left the scene. After leaving the location, I sat down and again reviewed the recordings. The messages clearly fit the history of the home and its tragedies.

Of course, details of the case had made the news originally and were widely known. Documentaries were made chronicling the entire series of events that culminated in the terrible deaths associated with the family and home.

One documentary I found fascinating detailed the experiences of a different family living in the home years later who reported negative activity occurring in the house. A psychic medium was called in to evaluate the haunting. The psychic felt that although the man had killed his wife and caused the death of his daughter, his spirit still refused to take accountability for his actions. Furthermore, it seemed his spirit was holding the other family members back, preventing them from crossing over into the light and the afterlife because of his own fear of the consequences he may face.

Trapped together as a group, the spirits continued to be consumed by negative emotions generated from the horrific acts that occurred.

The whole scenario played over and over in my head. This was such a disturbing situation. Not only were there the sad deaths of several people, but in reflecting on the psychic's information, and coupling it with the EVPs we had recorded, I could now see the souls of these people were in torment. It was a horrible thing to contemplate.

Growing up Catholic, the lessons of the church were ingrained in me and my empathy for the mother and daughter was intense. I also considered the possible consequences the soul of the murderer could face in the afterlife.

I couldn't stop thinking about the trapped spirits of the two women and I kept wondering if there was something I could do to aid them. Then it came to me. From the time I was young, my father, who was especially devout, always kept little bottles of holy water all over the house. Thinking about what I could do to help the trapped spirits, my mind went immediately to the idea of using some blessed water. Perhaps I could help the mother and daughter, at least find some peace if they were truly trapped on the property.

Bottle of holy water in hand, Gregory and I returned to the property one night around midnight.

We parked on the street and I got out of the car. The neighborhood was quiet, and I didn't want to disturb anyone, but I was feeling very determined. I approached the home and went to the side of the house where there was a flight of steps. I was moving on instinct and faith.

Opening the holy water, I began to throw it out of the bottle in the shape of a cross while stating aloud:

"In the name of Jesus Christ! If anything evil here is trapping the mother and daughter, let them go in peace."

I stated the words as a command, with confidence.

Looking back, I realize this was not something I should have attempted at the time. As a beginning investigator, I was not fully prepared or trained to undertake such a course of action. Religious provocation carries certain risks with it and should only be done by those fully ready to undertake such actions.

As human beings, we can't force spirits to cross over, we can only encourage them to accept unconditional love and forgiveness from God. Showing lost souls the path to the other side, presenting them with the knowledge and opportunity to cross over and continue their journey can be rewarding actions.

Despite my lack of preparation, I was compelled by something to press forward that night at the house. Perhaps it was my intuition telling me I needed to help, perhaps it was a matter of the intense energy I felt and the connection to the pain being experienced by those spirits. From a personal view, if I was trapped in such a state, I would want someone to try and help me find peace.

Ironically, the entire incident set the precedent for my path in the paranormal. As I moved forward over the years, saying prayers, using holy water, and attempting to help lost or trapped spirits has proven to be a constant theme in my life.

But as I would find, the effects from this night were far from over.

I returned to my normal routine, working, music and thinking about my next steps in the paranormal. I hoped I'd had some positive influence on the souls trapped at the home, but of course there was no way to be certain at the time.

In the aftermath of that night, something changed in my life. Within a week or two of using the holy water at the home, I started to notice an odd feeling. I started to feel like someone was following me. The experience was constant, whether I was at home, work, or out doing other things. I can't begin to express the strange intensity of this experience. At times, it felt as if there was someone there physically, and I would look around expecting to see a flesh and blood person. I quickly realized I was dealing with something more, something paranormal in nature.

I finally sat down and tried to determine exactly what was going on. I needed to know if this was something malicious in nature.

I started my recorder and asked a question:

"Is someone following me?"

The response took me by surprise to say the least:

"I am the daughter. You freed me from my stepfather's hell. Thank you."

I hardly knew how to react. I wanted to believe I had indeed helped set the woman free, but I was also aware that the demonic likes to play tricks and ply on people's egos and emotions.

I felt uneasy considering all the possibilities. Had I really freed a trapped spirit? Or was something dark and sinister now following me in an attempt to interfere with my life.

I decided to continue gathering evidence and guard myself while doing so. If the woman was following me for some reason, I needed to learn why and hopefully help her cross over the rest of the way and continue her soul's journey.

While at work in the wine store one day, a woman came in to make a purchase. She had her eight-year-old son with her. Standing in the store, the boy suddenly turned to his mother and proclaimed:

"There is a ghost there."

The boy was looking in my direction and the hair went up on the back of my neck. From the mouths of babes had come additional confirmation that a spirit was following me.

I was unsure exactly how to deal with what was unfolding. Over the following weeks, Gregory and I continued our explorations of reportedly haunted locations. Collecting EVPs from a variety of sites.

As we continued to investigate, another twist presented itself. Apparently the spirit of the woman attached to me was responding to questions I asked at other locations. The female voice was consistent, and I always quickly recognized it.

Standing one day in a haunted cemetery, I posed a question in front of a headstone:

"Are you still here with us?"

Rather than a response from the deceased, the spirit of the woman, who I'll now call "Chrissy" answered:

"Sean, they have crossed over."

Such things became a constant. Wherever I went to investigate, if I asked questions of the spirits there, Chrissy would answer.

The messages also started to give me more direct information related to my blessing of the house. One message from Chrissy stated:

"My stepfather is very angry with what you've done."

It was unsettling to know I had angered a negative spirit. What would I have to deal with as a result of attempting to aid the souls of the women?

I always prayed a lot, but now I started making a greater habit of saying regular prayers. I would pray each night before going to bed in order to invoke more protection. I didn't regret my actions, but I was still deeply concerned over what potential problems I could face.

I began to realize that my conversations with Chrissy in this format were helping me understand the mechanics of a medium's abilities.

One night, I discovered, upon playback of a recording, the woman's spirit was answering me *before* I physically asked the question!

Was she hearing me telepathically?

Spirits are known to communicate this way, but the experience was new for me. The messages made sense, so at least I knew I wasn't going crazy.

Chrissy's presence in my life went on for two months. I was both intrigued and somewhat puzzled by the continued presence of the woman's spirit. While I had done all I could to help her cross over, I still found it odd that she had become so connected to me.

But another strange synchronicity would bring me further revelations. It was my sister who helped put the pieces together. Sitting around talking one day, the topic of the tragic deaths came up. My sister began talking about the young woman who had taken her own life and how she was connected to people we knew.

Despite having researched the events and the family, until this moment, sitting and talking with my sister, I had not put "two and two together." I asked her to repeat the woman's name and the people she was connected to. A strange feeling of recognition came over me and I quickly opened my computer to look at my Facebook page.

I couldn't believe what I quickly confirmed. A couple of months before the woman had committed suicide off the bridge, she had added me as a friend on Facebook. Although I did not know her personally at the time, we had a number of friends in common, so I accepted her friend request. When I did, she sent me a brief personal message that said:

"Nice eyes."

Sitting in front of the screen, looking at her profile, I could hardly believe how the pieces had fallen together. Well before her death, this woman had reached out on a social level and contacted me. Who could have known things would unfold as they did? It was stunning. This was surreal in every way I could imagine.

My world had shifted yet again. I found myself communicating with Chrissy daily. It was as if I was living in two worlds at once. She even started giving me advice on mundane matters. She told me where to find my missing wallet for instance.

Other conversations with her were quite strange. One day, while trying to do an EVP session, my dog Murphy started whining. During playback of the session, I heard Chrissy's voice state:

"Bandit needs to go out."

The response was confusing, and I listened to it again to verify I had heard it correctly. My dog's name was Murphy, but when I was a child, I had a dog named Bandit. Why was she using that name? I asked the question to try to clarify. The response that came was:

"This is Bandit's soul reincarnated."

My family and I always thought Murphy looked a lot

like Bandit, and this information seemed to confirm there was something much more to it.

It's natural to question the fate of the spirits of animals. From my personal experience, I find that animals exude unconditional love and forgiveness. For me, dogs especially had always lived up to their nickname, "man's best friend."

If humans were heart-centered like most animals, we would live in a very different world.

One night while Gregory and I were at a local cemetery, things took a dark turn. We had walked around for some time, recording EVPs and paying attention to our senses. Out of nowhere, we both felt an intense pressure on our chests. It felt like a panic attack. My mind felt engulfed with overwhelming dread. It was something neither of us had ever experienced before. At first, we tried to diffuse the situation, but it only resulted in nervous laughter and further uneasiness. We quickly decided it was best to leave right away so we rushed to the car.

My recorder had been running the entire time we were at the cemetery. Eager to get to the bottom of our experience, we listened to the playback in the car.

Chrissy's voice came through. She was issuing a warning— about a demon.

This was a whole new level of concern.

After I returned home, I decided to ask Chrissy for more information.

"Why is there a demon? What does it have to do with us?"

"It is consumed with anger because you took a soul away."

Now I was really creeped out. What exactly had I stumbled into, and what might I be going up against?

During the months I was having a dialogue with Chrissy, more of my spiritual abilities awakened. I'd had visions and received information on a variety of levels. In one vision, Chrissy herself was there and told me I should avoid cemeteries, because there was a demon waiting for an opportunity to hurt me. Cemeteries, she said, were a prime spot where I may be attacked.

Gregory and I were both a bit freaked out at all of the information coming forth. He was more skeptical in general, and had doubted some of my experiences in the past. Hearing this however, he took on a very different tone. We both knew this was all too real.

A few nights later things grew even more intense. I was lying in bed when I saw a shadow figure come out of a mirror in my room. A wave of terror passed over me—I was paralyzed. Was I dreaming? Was this sleep paralysis?

I watched as the shadow came over my chest, feeling the pressure of the thing, whatever it was, when with a jolt I woke up.

I was drenched in sweat and my body covered with cold chills.

At work the next morning, I told Gregory about my experience.

He too had experienced a strange night and related it to me:

"I had a dream we were in a cemetery under water. I woke up feeling like I was being choked."

Both of us having such negative experiences on the same night wasn't a coincidence. I was now sure that something, something dark, had us in its sights. The question remained, what were we dealing with?

Was it the spirit of the stepfather, the murderer, angry that I had tried to help the trapped spirits of his family? Or was it, as Chrissy had warned, something truly demonic?

I decided to return again to the cemetery, this time with my sister in tow. I didn't expect anything negative to manifest with the sun shining on us, but I was wrong. EVPs recorded that day yielded a range of screams, threats and vulgar profanities. The spirit identified itself as the stepfather and the same heavy pressure fell again on my chest. So did the feelings of panic. The conditions remained with me until we left the location.

I was wary of returning at any point, especially at night, but Gregory convinced me I should return, as long as I carried additional protection.

I set off once again, this time in addition to a bottle of holy water, I carried a big crucifix. In the interim, I learned the protection prayer of the Archangel Saint Michael. The prayer is short, but powerful, and since that night, it has remained a constant tool in my arsenal. In fact, to this day, I recite the prayer each night before turning in because of the powerful protection I believe I receive from it.

"Archangel Saint Michael, defend us in battle against the wickedness and snares of the devil. May God rebuke him, we humbly pray, and do thou O Prince of the Heavenly Host by the divine power of God, cast into hell Satan and all the evil spirits that roam throughout the world seeking the ruin of souls.

Amen."

Somewhat reluctantly, we entered the cemetery that night. Striding to the middle of the property, an unexpected thing happened. There was no negativity. No pressure on the chest, no creepy vibes. In fact, if anything, it felt peaceful.

I started my recorder and asked why things were so different. The response gave me chills:

"There are angels around us and they look beautiful."

Was this due to the prayers I had recited prior to visiting the cemetery? I felt validated, and in that moment the strength of my faith increased, rising higher than I ever imagined it could. I felt deeply connected in a profound, spiritual way to God and my pursuit to help as many souls as I could.

Following this experience I continued having visions. I had one of Chrissy telling me I had angered Satan and that I needed to be very careful.

In another, she was in a cabin near a beautiful waterfall. She looked at me and spoke:

"Since you freed me from that dark place and called upon angels, they are deciding what to do with me. Some of our relatives are close by."

It was a warm feeling knowing she was in a different place and that I had played some role in helping her get there.

After this vision, I knew my time communicating with her was drawing to a close. I vividly remember the last time I spoke with her.

My sister Danielle and I were sharing an apartment in New York. She had experienced a lot of unusual things herself and I always told her about my adventures and experiences pursuing the paranormal. It was a lot to swallow — angels, spirits, demons— but she always listened as I recounted my ride on this crazy wave.

One night Danielle and I were recording some EVPs. Chrissy's voice came through as it so often did, and during the evening she made a number of statements:

"The angels are fighting the abomination over my soul."

"The angels are going to take me to heaven."

"I want to think you for helping my soul find this peace."

"You need to be careful, the evil one will try to deceive you."

"I know you're strong. I am leaving and wanted to say goodbye."

A rush of emotions came over me. My sister and I both started crying. I had never felt anything like I did that night.

After the last recording played, I felt lost. For two solid months Chrissy had been with me. We communicated daily like the closest of friends. Now that she was gone, I felt empty and scared. So often she had warned me when I was in danger. Now I was afraid of being attacked by unseen forces.

I looked up protection prayers and recited all the ones I could find. I slept with my crucifix over my chest, concerned that the shadow figure would manifest again, or that something else would attempt to overtake me. I realized I had stepped in the way of evil and chances were I would be a target the rest of my life.

After a sleepless night I dragged myself to work the next morning. I felt beaten and battered as well as exhausted. My mind wouldn't stop wondering if Chrissy was still with me by any chance. I couldn't stop thinking about trying to contact her.

I snuck into the basement of the store and pulled out my recorder to do a quick EVP session in an attempt to make contact. I asked if Chrissy was still with me. The response was a creepy voice that dripped with malicious energy:

"Sean…I'm still here."

It was a female voice, but I knew right away it wasn't Chrissy. Someone, or something was trying to mimic her and convince me she was still present. "It" wanted me to continue with communications.

I was distraught and spiritually drained. I turned off the recorder and went back to work.

For a time I experienced a kind of withdrawal. I began to realize how connected I had become to Chrissy's spirit and how—to an unhealthy degree—I had come to depend on her messages.

I had been giving so much attention and commitment to the spirit world that I had strayed from the physical world, in a sense. This was a powerful lesson, as this is dangerous territory. It can take a toll on the mind, body and spirit.

Back at work after my quick EVP attempt in the basement, I found the woman with the odd little eight-year-old boy back in the store. Since he had pointed out a ghost before, I wondered to myself, "What in the world is this kid going to say this time?"

I quickly found out. The kid walked straight over to me, pointed over my head and stated:

"Look Mom, look at the big huge blue moon over his head."

I was startled. There was nothing behind me that could have given this kid any kind of impression of a light, not to mention a "blue moon." I knew in that moment that the boy had seen a ball of spirit energy, or an orb, over me.

After the pair left the store, I went to the computer and looked up the meaning of a large blue orb. I found out that a big, blue ball of spirit energy was something commonly associated with the Archangel Saint Michael and the appearance of the orb meant he was watching over you and protecting you.

I sat back, chilled to the bone. I felt another wave of peace flowing over me and a renewed faith in God and my beliefs. Here, I was sure, was a sign of the validity of my actions and a message that angels were indeed protecting me. And not just any angel, but by no less than Saint Michael himself.

That day I ordered a pendant of Saint Michael stepping on a demon and dedicated myself to him, with the clear intent to do all I could under the guidance of God, my faith and Saint Michael the protector.

From the time I received the Saint Michael medal, it has never left my neck.

To this day, there are still stories that circulate about what I call the murder/suicide house. People living in the home have purportedly been scratched, cleaning people have reported seeing apparitions and experiencing cold chills in one of the bedrooms. Others report an odd feeling of being watched while in the home.

My first full paranormal case had transformed me forever.

CHAPTER FIVE:
Visions of Ed Warren

After I had helped Chrissy cross over and shaken off the startling change in my life, I discovered I had an even deeper passion for the paranormal. Since I had taken the step to interfere in the plans of dark forces and entities, I knew there was no turning back anyway, so it was time to forge ahead.

I continued to have dreams and premonitions about coming events. One night, I had a dream that the father of one of my close friends was in the hospital. I told my friend about it the next day, but he laughed it off, not believing in such things. A few days later, his father collapsed in their home. Prompted by what I had told him, my friend didn't hesitate to call 911 believing the matter to be a serious one. Fortunately, his father recovered from the incident.

Gregory and I continued to investigate locations as we could find them. After my previous encounters, I found I was drawn to learn more about the demonic and negative hauntings so that I was better prepared. I started reading more books about the paranormal, especially ones that delved into the darker side.

One book that had a great impact on me was "The Demonologist" by Ed and Lorraine Warren. The Warren's have become more well known in recent years because of the movie franchise "The Conjuring," which is based on their real-life cases. The Warrens had a long history of investigating the paranormal though. The Warrens were pioneers in the field and reading "The Demonologist," I found myself glued to the book, fascinated by their cases.

Ed passed away in 2006, so sadly I never had a chance to meet him in person. I have met Lorraine and visited the Warren's legendary museum where many of the haunted objects they gathered over the years are stored.

Ed was also a painter, and he was known to paint pictures of houses known to be haunted as a way to connect with the home owners and gain entry to the home to investigate. He also painted scenes from various cases the couple worked on. Many of these paintings are on display in the Warren's Museum.

One night, I had what I believe was a visitation from Ed. It was clear and vivid. In the vision, Ed sat me down in his living room. Getting comfortable in his chair, he looked at me and stated:

"Sean, sit down and tell me what's going on in your life. I would love to paint one of your scary stories."

I was intrigued and asked him which story he would like to paint.

"Yes, now hold on a second, something weird is happening."

Ed stood up and walked over to an old black rotary phone and picked up the receiver.

I came out of the vision at that point and sat there thinking about the details. I could clearly remember the way Ed was dressed. A thin, maroon colored sweater with the white collar of a shirt visible beneath it, and khaki pants.

Right after having this vision, I made my first visit to the Warren's museum. It was for an event so there were several other people present. We were escorted into the living room, and it looked identical to the room in my vision where I spoke to Ed. We sat in rows of chairs and waited. After a moment Lorraine came in and sat down in the corner chair, the same one Ed had sat in during my vision.

Lorraine told the story of how she and Ed met and talked

about the highlights of some of their cases and experiences. Footage of an exorcism being performed was then presented, it was disturbing and fascinating at the same time.

Speaking with Lorraine Warren.

Once the presentation was over, we entered the museum to view the collection of haunted items from around the world. Included in the collection is the infamous doll, Annabelle.

After the official event was over, there was a meet and greet with Lorraine and her son-in-law, Tony Spera. At this point, I had a chance to speak with Lorraine and asked what advice she had for a budding medium with newly discovered abilities. She recommended keeping a notebook on hand to record notes of my visions. I also had a chance to relate my experience with Ed to her and Tony.

Tony noted the description of the clothing matched the way Ed used to dress. He also said the language sounded like Ed's way of speaking. Tony also told me Ed liked to use an old black rotary phone all the time, it was kept right outside the museum.

Though it may sound minor, it was nice to hear outside confirmation of things I was experiencing in my visions.

Following this, there were a few other synchronicities and visions involving Ed Warren. A psychic friend of mine told me he saw Ed's spirit around me. Reportedly, Ed stated:

"We have mutual friends. We are leaves off the same tree."

This same psychic told me:

"Look out for a coin with the same face on both sides."

I wasn't sure what to make of the statement, but a few days later, when getting change back from a purchase, I discovered a quarter with a red cross painted on both sides. I kept the coin as a representation of synchronicity, and as a statement on the importance of listening to information from trusted sources. There are many people who claim psychic ability, but not all of them have genuine ability. It takes time and discernment to learn who you can trust in terms of intuitive information.

I soon experienced another vision involving Ed. I was in the back seat of a car with Lorraine. She was wearing a plaid skirt and it looked like we were in the 1970's.

Ed was in the driver's seat and was shouting, *"We are off to the Amityville house."*

Anyone with even minor interest in the paranormal has likely heard of the infamous Amityville house, location of the murders of an entire family in 1974. The Long Island, New York home is the site where Ronald DeFeo Jr. killed his parents and his four siblings.

Later, when the Lutz family moved into the home, they purportedly experienced extreme demonic activity. The Warrens had investigated the home previously and it became one of their most notorious cases.

As my vision continued, we arrived at the Amityville home and walked inside. Ed turned to me and said:

"Sean, you know we're back in time now?"

I responded that I didn't know, and Ed pointed over to the top floor saying:

"Take a look up there Sean."

As I looked up I saw a huge banner with the word "accolade" written on it.

Ed then told me:

"You are part of all of this, just so you know."

The vision ended, and I came out of it wondering what it all meant. I wasn't familiar with the word accolade, so I looked it up. The definition stated:

"An award or privilege granted as a special honor or as an acknowledgement of merit, also a bestowing of knighthood."

I wasn't sure how to make sense of it all. Perhaps, I thought, it had something to do with my future involvement in the paranormal. Curiously, this vision occurred the day before the premiere of "The Conjuring," a movie I was excited to see.

I came to feel the idea of an accolade meant simply doing my best to help trapped souls and those tormented by dark forces.

I continued to read all I could about dark and demonic hauntings. "Shadows of the Dark" by John Zaffis was another influence on me. John is the nephew of Ed Warren and he's known as the "Godfather of the Paranormal."

The third title that made a lot of impact on me was "The Dark Sacrament," a book about demonic hauntings and possessions in Ireland by David Kiely and his wife Christina McKenna.

Along the way I gained an understanding of the stages of demonic hauntings, broken down into three levels:

One—Infestation. This is when a demonic spirit gains access to a location by invitation. When this occurs, the demon will begin to manifest negative things in the home and the lives of the people living there. This often quickly leads to the next stage.

Two—Oppression. This is when demonic forces start to take a psychological toll on victims, attempting to break them mentally, physically and spiritually. Negative emotions are pushed; anger, sadness and depression become the norm. Ultimately, demonic forces try to push victims to harm themselves and those around them in any way possible. If this continues for a period of time, it can lead to the third and most dangerous stage.

Three—Possession. At this final stage, the demon has broken the spirit of its victim and begins to take over the physical body of its target. At this point, the victim is usually so worn down and beaten they simply give in. This is the most extreme level of demonic activity in our physical world.

CHAPTER SIX:
Leviathan

Although I knew I was protected by Saint Michael, I still had the sense of being a target of negative entities. During some investigations, a recurring voice kept referring to itself as "Leviathan."

Leviathan is a demonic creature named in the bible. It's a sea creature with seven heads. The demon's name is from old Hebrew and means "whale," hence the depictions of the monster as an aquatic beast.

The oldest version of Leviathan is found in the Babylonian creation story, where the storm god Marduk battles and defeats the sea monster Tiamat. More modern translations of the creature view it as a dragon.

In the Christian bible, the battle between God and the beast Leviathan is referenced several times, for instance this passage from Psalms:

"You broke divided the sea by Your strength; You broke the heads of the sea serpents in the waters. You broke the heads of Leviathan in pieces and gave him as food to the people inhabiting the wilderness."

Psalms 74: 13-14, American Patriot's Bible

According to most of the early tales, Leviathan is a beast of flesh and blood. It roamed the oceans, could breathe fire, and smoke streamed from its nostrils. St. Thomas Aquinas named Leviathan the demon of envy.

Another nickname for Leviathan is "hell mouth" because of drawings of the creature showing it with a large, gaping maul.

Around the time Leviathan's name started coming through on EVP recordings, I had another intense experience.

I had a vision of myself walking out of the bedroom and to the bathroom. I knew I was dreaming. As I looked up into the mirror, I felt something grab my head and slam it against the mirror. When my face hit the mirror, my body—still in bed—went into sleep paralysis.

I heard a terrifying voice that sounded half female and half animal. It reverberated loudly when it spoke.

"*I see you*" the strange voice said.

I awoke very shaken. Looking at the clock, I noted the time was three a.m., known to some as the "witching hour," a time when dark entities are extremely active. Some Christians believe the hour between three and four a.m. is opposite of the time when Jesus was crucified.

As if the vivid dream/vision wasn't disturbing enough, there was a follow up to it. A week after the experience I was in the shower. I usually shave while standing in the shower, and as I looked over to my shaving mirror, I saw a message spelled out in the steam collected on the mirror.

"*I see U.*"

The "U" was written very large. Clearly, something was getting a message through to tell me once again I was in the crosshairs.

After this incident there were others. At times I would hear a sound in my bedroom that sounded like a lion roaring. On other occasions, I heard a voice shout:

"*You are nothing!*"

I knew this was an evil manifestation, trying to get to me

in whatever way it could, purportedly to intimidate or deter me from doing my work. I continued to say my protective prayers each night and used holy water whenever I felt the energy was getting negative or too intense.

I had other experiences too. I dreamed about what appeared to be a little girl, trying to pull my astral body away from my physical form, and taunting me to *"come play with me."* This happened on numerous occasions.

On yet another night, I fell asleep on the couch and found myself in a dark torture chamber. There was a creature with scales and yellow, cat-like eyes watching and growling from the shadows.

My body was again locked in a state of sleep paralysis. This time I was able to quickly snap out of it. When I did, I came back to a full, wakened state only to see a green apparition of some sort right beside the couch where I had fallen asleep.

This was a new element and I did some research in hopes of figuring out what this strange sight meant. I found that some Catholics believe a green-colored manifestation was a sign of the demon of envy, none other than Leviathan. Again, synchronicities were lining up and things were making sense in a strange way.

My apartment was blessed on a regular basis, and I even put two St. Benedict coins under my bed for further protection while I slept. To think these dark entities could still manifest under such conditions was another indication to me of how potent and powerful evil can be. I understood yet again the need for constant vigilance.

CHAPTER SEVEN:
Angels & Family Spirits

It's important to note that not every paranormal experience was a terrifying case. Sometimes there are manifestations that affirm the positive and show us protective spirits are present. Such was the case one day when I decided to take a picture at the back door of my local church. When I looked at the photo, I saw what appeared to be the face of an angel. It was guarding the door with a glowing spear.

I find it comforting to know that holy places have their own protectors standing guard, further adding to the spiritual strength of the place and making it a sanctuary for those in need.

Positive energy can be seen around people too, and I've noticed this with close friends and family members at times.

One Christmas, I went to the cemetery in Eastchester, New York where my grandparents are buried. My father was with me, and together we said a prayer for my grandparents.

I took out my camera to take some photos. I was about thirty feet away from my father and took a picture of him while he was praying over a grave.

It was just starting to get dark. A yellow spot light was originating from the sky right over my father. It was an amazing manifestation.

My father is the most selfless person I've ever met in my life. He would literally give the shirt off his back to anyone in need. There's no doubt in my mind or heart where he will go once he leaves this plane of existence. I took the light in the photo as a positive sign, and acknowledgement of my father and all the good he has done in his life.

*   *   *

My cousin Lisa is an open-minded person with an interest in the paranormal. I always enjoy family gatherings at her home. I was at Lisa's house for a special occasion one afternoon. It was a birthday party for Lisa's daughter, Mary.

Looking around at all the decorations it was easy to tell that Mary was a big fan of Hello Kitty. The popular character was everywhere in the room. Nine family members were gathered for the party, and we sat down in chairs arranged in a circle. Lisa was sitting next to me. Several things happened at once.

I caught a sudden whiff of what smelled like my deceased grandmother's distinct perfume. Interestingly, Lisa's daughter is named after my grandmother Mary. At the same time, Lisa asked me if I thought grandma or grandpa were with us for the celebration. As soon as the question was asked, the light over our heads started to flicker. I smiled and answered, "Yes, it's a good possibility they are."

As all of this was transpiring, a toy car with a Hello Kitty motif on it was sitting on it's side in front of me. When Lisa asked the question, the car started to rev its motor as if it was going to take off!

I picked the toy up and placed it on its wheels. I then asked:

"Grandma or grandpa, if you're here, can you move the car towards Lisa?"

Sure enough, the little car started to move towards my cousin. Lisa was startled at the incident and the quick response from the toy. She told the rest of the family present what had happened. Of course the responses were mixed. Some of my family members aren't quite as open minded about messages from the other side.

Nevertheless, I enjoyed the evening immensely. After the flickering lights and the movements of the toy car, Lisa and I decided to slip off and try an EVP session to see if we could get any direct responses from our relatives.

Sitting by ourselves in another, quiet room, I started my recorder and we asked my grandparents if they could move the car again, this time towards my other cousin, Suzanne.

The car was still in the other room with the rest of the family. There were audible gasps as the car backed up, did a three-point turn, and rolled forward directly towards Suzanne.

Suzanne's husband is a skeptic and led the charge asking if there was a remote control for the car and who was hiding out making the car act on command.

The remote was quickly located—still wrapped in its original plastic and still in the box the toy had come in. On further inspection, it was verified the remote didn't even have batteries in it, ruling out its use to manipulate the car.

As a further test, Lisa and I stepped out of the room again and this time, asked grandma and grandpa to move the toy car towards Uncle Jim.

Jim was sitting in the corner of the room and again, the car backed up, turned, this time to the right, and made a beeline straight for Uncle Jim.

Uncle Jim loudly proclaimed he needed another drink, while the skeptic found himself speechless.

Sometimes, I think, the spirits just like to have a little fun.

CHAPTER EIGHT:
Scratches in the Cemetery

Eastchester, New York was originally settled in 1664 by ten families that migrated from Connecticut. At the outbreak of the American Revolution, Eastchester was a peaceful farming community. While no battles were fought in the town, it still has a long and rich history.

Gregory and I headed to Eastchester's cemetery, "Holy Mount" to do some investigating one evening. There was a personal connection for me because Holy Mount is the same cemetery my grandparents are buried in.

It was chilly that evening, around forty degrees, but as we walked through the cemetery snapping photos, I felt like I had entered a sauna. The energy became so heavy I could barely stand. I bent over, putting my hands on my knees and tried to breathe. I couldn't speak for about ten seconds.

Gregory was asking me if I was alright and what was happening. I composed myself and told him what I was feeling. Using my senses, I tried to guide us to the source of the heavy energy. When I found it, I pointed the spot out to Gregory. He took a few strides to the spot and put his hand out over the area I had designated.

"It feels like a fire is burning where my hand is!" He exclaimed.

After he made the statement, Gregory reported a burning sensation on his stomach. He lifted his shirt and we saw a set of what appeared to be claw marks across his stomach.

I was stunned at the sight. It's one thing to see this kind of physical contact and manifestation on television, but quite another to witness it yourself. It was certainly the highlight of the evening's investigation and was yet another defining moment for me personally.

Although Holy Mount is a small cemetery, there was frequent paranormal activity, so we returned on many occasions. One night proved to be yet another learning experience.

As soon as we got out of the car, I noticed the air felt thick. Something didn't feel right at all.

Right away, Gregory started to provoke, stating:

"Whatever is around, scratch me."

I didn't feel good about Gregory prodding the spirits this way. As it turned out, he had indulged in a few drinks after work, since he'd had an especially bad day. Let me be clear, I don't for a moment believe it's a good idea to drink alcohol and then investigate at a haunted location, it's a very bad mix and potentially opens a person up to the influence of negative entities. I personally would never take such a risk, but as for others, all I can do is offer my opinion. I told Gregory I didn't think what he was doing was a good idea. Still, he persisted in his actions that night.

I was using an app on my smartphone. The app, called "Ghost Radar" measures energy near the phone and utilizes GPS and wi-fi signals. In theory, spirits can manipulate the energy and "speak" using the words held in the app's database. The app is similar to the more well-known Ovilus device.

A lot of people are skeptical about using an application on a phone in an investigation. In my opinion, a spirit can manipulate anything electrical—lights, televisions, and yes, cell phones.

It's healthy to be objective about any type of equipment you use on an investigation. Being sensitive to the energy of spirits, I like to use equipment to confirm what my other senses are picking up at any given location.

As we continued to walk around, Gregory continued to provoke, and I ran Ghost Radar. The app displayed the word "Satan." At that time, Gregory started having a burning sensation on the side of his stomach.

It was pitch black that night and very difficult for us to see each other, even while close together. I used the light on my cell phone as Gregory lifted his shirt to see if he'd been scratched again. Sure enough, he had. This time the marks were long and wide. They were so bright, they looked like lipstick and ran from his breast all the way down to his waist. I took a photo and then showed it to Gregory. He was dumbstruck, and the sight of the scratches led him to issue another challenge:

"Why don't you do it to me again?"

At his statement, the app responded with the word "inhuman" and Gregory felt a burning sensation on his arm. As soon as I put the light on his arm, we saw a set of scratch marks identical to the ones on his stomach.

While this was occurring, I felt a burning sensation on my back in the shoulder area. When we checked, there were no scratch marks to be found, though the burning feeling persisted. Was my St. Michael pendant protecting me? I decide to try to confirm if that was the case.

"Are you trying to scratch me but can't because I am protected?"

This question caused an amazing response via EVP. A voice blurted out two sentences in quick succession:

"St. Michael is watching him."

"It's his fucking pendant!"

Over time I had many experiences in Holy Mount cemetery. It became one of my classrooms in a sense, since there was such a wide variety of activity there. At times the place felt peaceful, but other times I would find my equilibrium thrown off just by walking around the grounds.

The location is also where I would frequently have visions. They didn't always make sense or connect with the location itself, at least in a literal way.

One night I saw a vision of children sitting between two trees, they appeared to be doing a magical ritual of some kind and were using a Ouija board. I translated the vision as meaning someone had attempted to open a portal on the cemetery grounds. I knew this could also explain the heavy energy and manifestations Gregory and I had experienced while investigating the location.

One night while exploring the cemetery by myself, I had a vision of a creature. It had long arms and legs, three fingers and three toes, and long black fingernails. I felt it was some type of demonic minion that worked for an even more sinister force.

My head was pounding, and the atmosphere became oppressive. I felt a swirling sensation around me, and I started to say prayers of protection. Soon after, the feeling dissipated. I decided it was time to leave the site before things became heavy again.

I returned the next night, this time I had my holy water in hand and I felt more prepared for what may be lurking at the location. As soon as I arrived my head started pounding as it had the night before.

I walked through the cemetery and over to the two trees I had seen in my previous vision. My head was throbbing with pain, but I pushed forward and took out my holy water. Throwing the blessed water around the area, I began reciting prayers. The distinct smell of my grandmother's perfume came to me in that moment, and I wondered if she was there, helping me and watching over me.

After blessing the area I believed to be the center of negative energy, I walked back in the direction of my car. The pains I was experiencing were almost unbearable. My head throbbed and my body ached. I yelled out:

"In the name of Jesus Christ, back off, I do not give permission for any evil spirit to touch me or attack me."

Ten feet away from me, there was a flash of something, I looked up and saw a shadow figure. The thing was eight feet tall and blacker than the night itself. I was chilled to the bone looking at it, and as I stood there in shock, a long, nasty growl came out of the spirit box I was holding.

An eight-foot-tall shadow figured appeared.
(Illustration by Kimberly Carper)

I was running the app on my phone at the same time. It had been quiet so far, but now it suddenly said the word "legion."

My equipment froze. Both the spirit box and my cell phone simply locked up and wouldn't function. I decided it was time to leave again. I couldn't take the chance that I might be vulnerable to negative entities, so I headed for my car while reciting prayers of protection. I reached my vehicle, blessed it with holy water, jumped in and drove out of there.

I couldn't quite shake the feeling of seeing the large shadow creature. My mind raced over the details I was able to discern. It seemed to be wearing a hood and held something, perhaps a large sword, that was pointed to the ground. On another level, I felt as though the thing knew me and knew who I was. It was unsettling to be on the radar of something that felt so sinister.

During this period, I began doing live broadcasts of my investigations on a platform called "Periscope." These broadcasts were streamed right from my cell phone and it added a new aspect to my time at haunted locations—now people could watch from a distance and interact with me while I was at a location.

It was some time before I returned to Holy Mount cemetery. About two months after my encounter with the shadow creature, I returned to the site to conduct another investigation.

I turned on the spirit box and the app on my cell phone and asked if there were any spirits present who would like to communicate.

The first word that came out was *"British."* I wasn't sure of the relevance at that time and continued to ask questions and see what other evidence I could get. As I was sitting there with my equipment I noticed someone coming through the cemetery entrance. The person was dressed in red and I assumed they were coming to pay respects at a family member's grave. I turned the equipment off. The white noise from the spirit box can be rather loud, and I always like to show proper respect, especially in a cemetery. I continued the periscope feed and told viewers I would resume working with the devices as soon as the visitor had left. As I was sitting there, I began to wonder why the person had walked up to the entrance. The cemetery is on a hill and it's about a quarter of a mile walk to reach it. I'd never seen anyone walk up there, they always drove since the road is a dead end.

I looked back towards the entrance but didn't see the person anywhere. I walked over to see if I could locate them, the site is not that large, and visibility is good. There was no one around. I stood there scratching my head wondering what had happened.

My eyes searched the entire cemetery. When I again turned back towards the entrance, I saw the person in red again. There was a glint from what looked like gold buttons on the jacket, but the person's face was blurry and indistinguishable. The figure was walking from left to right away from the entrance where I had originally seen it, then it disappeared.

I was speechless. I realized I was still on periscope and told the viewers what I had seen. Then I turned on the spirit box and asked about what I saw. The reply quickly came back:

"It was a soldier. It was a spirit. It was real."

Someone watching the livestream reminded me that earlier the word "British" had come out of the app. Had I just witnessed the apparition of a British redcoat from the American Revolution?

The reality of the incident was still sinking in. I thought I was seeing a living, physical man enter the cemetery, yet there's no way a physical person could have vanished the way this figure did.

It was still light out and this was the first time I had seen such a thing—a ghost in full form. The experience has stayed with me to this day, and whenever I visit Holy Mount, I'm always on the lookout for that lone British soldier making his rounds.

CHAPTER NINE:
A Visit from my Former Boss

I had entered my second year of investigating the paranormal and more people were learning about my involvement. One girlfriend of mine decided to share a story with me that she believed was an omen of things to come.

When we were dating, I was living in a house with several roommates. She told me that she came over one day and witnessed something very frightening, something she had never told me before.

She said when she arrived at my house, she saw someone in a black cloak and hood standing outside, staring at my bedroom window. The figure terrified her, and when it turned to look at her, she saw a white face with black holes for eyes staring at her. The figured disappeared, leaving her very shaken. She never shared the story with me because she didn't want to sound crazy. Little did either of us know at the time, how many crazy experiences I would end up having.

As my life moved forward and I became involved in the paranormal, I have seen these hooded figures on numerous occasions. They are usually omens of coming events, so I'm always careful to call on additional protections when such things manifest around me.

One evening I had a vision of an angel standing beside me.

A sense of peace and calmness flooded over me. I heard the angel's voice, like a song, as it said:

"Peace be with you."

What followed was a personal message I wrote down as soon as I came out of the vision. I felt refreshed and renewed in my faith yet again.

The next day, I learned that a friend of mine had shown my photograph to a psychic. Not knowing anything about me, the psychic replied:

"He's a shadow chaser, he takes shadows and sends them back to where they belong."

* * *

When I was nineteen, I started college, but soon dropped out, choosing instead to pursue my career as a singer/songwriter. Music didn't pay the bills at the time, so I took a job for a husband and wife couple who owned a wine store. I would end up working at the same store off and on until the age of twenty-five.

My boss was an interesting guy. He had owned the wine store for thirty years, and had a deep passion for wine, from all its nuances to the business itself. At times he displayed quite a temper, and I never knew what his mood would be like when I came to work.

He was also known for sarcasm and he loved telling jokes. Sadly, it seemed he also battled depression, a serious thing for anyone to face.

He never had any kids and in hindsight, I think he and his wife regarded me as their surrogate son. They gave me nicknames including "puppy" and "drummer boy," because I was always pounding beats on my chest. It seemed like a silly habit to people around me, but I've done it for years as I play songs repeatedly in my mind. I was always writing a new tune.

Christmas time was our busiest and most profitable time of

year. From open to close, we always had a full line of customers throughout the holiday season. Our store also had a delivery service and I carted wine all around town, especially around the holidays. It was busy work, but I really didn't mind. It was nice to be out of the store and I could listen to music while I ran deliveries.

Stuck in his old ways, my boss would never relinquish any responsibilities. He also wasn't interested in new innovations or marketing strategies. Modernizing was simply not in his genes. His way had always worked, and that was fine by him. But as with many businesses, changing technology and stiff competition started taking a toll. Sales started to decline and the downward trend in his business contributed to his depression.

With crystal clarity, I remember my boss's last Christmas. It was 2010 and it had been a very long day. I'd had a lot of deliveries around town. After my last run, I drove my boss to his home. On the way, he started on one of his typical sarcastic rants.

"Fuck everything. I should just go home, take a gun, and blow my brains out."

It was a heavy statement but at the same time, he was laughing. This was typical of his way of talking, and because he was always making crazy statements, I didn't take it too seriously.

The holidays passed, and I was back to work at the store in January 2011. Towards the end of the month, I watched a documentary about demonic entities. It was full of information and prompted me to research more and more. It was slow at work and I was looking online for more details about something I'd heard in the program.

According to the show, each month had a demon assigned to it. I found it weird when I learned my birth month, February, was assigned to Leviathan, the same demonic name I had received repeatedly on various pieces of equipment.

At that time, my boss came over and saw what I was doing. He started in with his usual, telling me that angels and demons don't exist. When he looked closer and noticed I was researching what demons were assigned to each month, he leaned in to see what demon ruled his birth month. When he looked at the listing, he stood back up and shook his head.

"Well Sean, I guess I'm fucked. I was born in March, I was married in March and I opened this store in March."

As it turns out, the month of March is assigned to Satan himself. We laughed the whole thing off and continued our work for the day. Still, the information stayed with me and unlike my boss, I knew full well about the existence of both angels and demons. Learning that each month had a different demon attached to it was revealing. According to the information, the particular demon of a month would be more active during its assigned month.

After dealing with a long winter, I took a trip in late April to visit my mother. She was living in Panama City, Florida and I knew that getting to the beach would help revitalize me. Being near the water and palm trees was my ideal place, but there was another reason too. My aunt Cynnie was in poor health and my mother wanted my sister and I to come down for Easter so the family could be together.

It was only a three-day trip, too short in my opinion, but we enjoyed ourselves and the time with family. On the last day, I bought a bunch of food and told everyone to come over to my mothers for a barbecue.

That evening I kept getting calls from my boss back home. He rang my phone over and over and left a handful of messages. He wanted to confirm that I was definitely returning to work the following day.

I missed several of his calls and found it odd that he seemed so worried about my return. I finally got him on the phone and assured him I would be back at work on the following day as planned.

"Just make sure you're there. I need you there, Sean."

He was adamant. He and his wife were always nervous about coverage at the store, but it seemed a bit much, they were always able to depend on me. After speaking with him,

I thought nothing else about the matter and went back to time with my family.

Early the next morning, I boarded a plane and went back to New York. In no time at all, I was at work at the wine store. Fifteen minutes after I was there, three cops came storming into the store and headed straight to the back office looking for my boss's wife.

I felt a tightness in my gut and knew that whatever was going on, it was really bad. I reflected back on information that the spirit Chrissy had given me. She had told me my boss at the store was going to die within six months. I suddenly realized we were right around that time frame.

Thirty seconds after the cops entered the office, I heard my boss's wife let out a horrible groan. That sound is something you never want to hear in your life. The sound of someone realizing a loved one has died tragically.

The police officers came out of the office and one of them came over to confirm what I already knew. My boss was dead.

He was found in his bed where he had shot himself in the head.

In a flash, the Christmas conversation I'd had with him came flooding back. But this was no joking matter. Tragically, something within him had given up and he had taken his own life. I was numb. For all his quirks and sarcastic ways, I was really connected to the guy from knowing him so many years of my life.

In the days that followed, our regular customers learned the shocking news. He had met a lot of people during his thirty years running the store, and his wake was crowded with many of the people he'd met.

While at the wake I felt his presence around me. He'd known about my interest in the paranormal and always joked about it, but now he was on the other side, and I knew he'd be near me. Standing at a sink in the funeral home's bathroom, I had the feeling someone was watching me from the mirror. There was no one else in the room, so I took a photo. Later that night, I examined the pic closely and saw a reflection of my boss's face looking at me.

A few days after the funeral, I went to my boss's grave with Gregory and another coworker. I turned on my recorder and asked my boss if he was still there.

"Hey Sean" was the response. It was his clear, distinct voice. We were all taken aback, and I said some prayers before we left.

I continued working at the wine store, and on many occasions I would feel his presence. It was no surprise really, considering how much he loved the place and how much of his life had been spent there.

One night I was recording EVPs in the store after hours and received a clear response in my boss's voice.

"Sean, I saw the angels."

The response gave me chills. He always teased me and claimed he doubted the existence of angels, yet here was his voice confirming the existence of angelic beings.

There was other activity in the store, too. One night when I was closing up, I began to have a very strange feeling. I heard a noise in the back and started the video recorder on my cell phone, thinking I would perhaps capture something unusual.

Feeling the presence of my deceased boss again, I spoke out loud to him, asking him to step in front of my camera. In response, a grayish white anomaly the size of a baseball came flying past my camera screen in all directions. There were no bugs in the room and no dust was flying around, it was something truly anomalous.

I was also seeing this weird object in real time. Its shadow even blocked out the light briefly. I asked my boss if he could do the same thing again. In response, another perfectly spherical ball of energy appeared and dove in front of the camera before shooting off into the distance. It was an exciting thing to capture on video, but I didn't like the thought of my boss being stuck in the store for the afterlife.

I closed the shop and decided to head home. Standing in front of the store, I had the sudden urge to take some photos through the glass display windows. When I arrived home, I examined the photos closely. Sure enough, I had captured something. In one of the photos, I could see my boss's face staring out the window.

It's hard to imagine how to deal with such an intense loss. By Catholic tradition, suicide is a sin and the person committing it can be trapped in a horrible place. They may be trying to escape the pain they feel in their lives, but they risk trading that pain for something even worse.

There's a side note to the tragic death of my boss. It had always nagged at me, wondering where he had gotten a gun. It turned out, the answer contained some creepy information. My boss wanted a gun and had approached a friend of his who was a police officer. It so happened the cop had a gun he wanted to get rid of, so my boss got it from him. The creepy part? The cop wanted rid of the gun because his son had used it—to kill himself.

I can only imagine how much negative energy the suicide gun carried, and what if any affect it had on my boss, who was already depressed and fighting thoughts of killing himself.

The store was soon sold, and my boss's wife moved out of state, attempting no doubt to move on to the next part of her life.

In the course of these events, I had another vision, this one a lucid dream experience. In it I found myself in a room with a man. He had dark hair and a pale face. He looked at me and stated:

"This is the room I kill myself in over and over."

I jumped back to consciousness in a cold sweat.

After my boss's death, and the vision, I made it a regular habit to pray for those who had taken their own lives. I still pray for such souls on a regular basis, hoping they find and accept God's unconditional love and forgiveness.

The spirit of my boss still lingers. From time to time, I hear his voice, calling me by the nicknames he'd given me. He always had a good heart and I pray frequently for his soul in hopes that someday soon he can find peace and cross over into the light of heaven.

CHAPTER TEN:

The Black Horse Demon

In the spring of 2012, I was in Ohio to investigate a historic location called "Prospect Place." The site has a lot of diverse history and ties to the underground railroad. There has also been satanic activity on the property.

I arrived the night before and stayed in a nearby hotel. With the pending investigation, I had a vision that was very disturbing.

I saw Pope Benedict XVI. He was on a parade float and waving. Oddly, there was no one there to greet him, and the float seemed to move in slow motion. Still, he waved his hand to the left and to the right as if there were crowds of people around.

A priest came over and stood next to me. He was dressed in casual black clothes and he spoke to me.

"Sean, you know that's not the real Pope, right?"

"Really? Is that so?" I responded.

I shifted around to my right and looked up. There was a huge statue of Satan facing away from me. The statue turned towards me, revealing wide, glowing eyes. The stone statue transformed into a large black horse with red eyes with smoke exhaling from its nostrils. The thing radiated evil. It stood up on its hind legs and stomped its hooves down, then it took off into the darkness. I woke up, shaken from the experience.

Curiously, this was the only vision I had with Pope Benedict and in less than a year, he had resigned from his position without any explanation.

The next day, I was up and out of the hotel and headed for our investigation. When we arrived at Prospect Place, the first thing I noticed was a little black pole with a black horse head on top of it. The pole was just to the right of the front stairs and I was quickly reminded of my unnerving dream from the night before.

We were shown in to the location and started setting up equipment for the night. This would be my first full overnight investigation and I was anxious to get started.

As the sun set, a fog crept over the area and engulfed the open field near the house. It was eerie and added to the creep factor of the location.

Things got started very quickly at Prospect Place. Taking a walk on the grounds, I heard a low growl directed at me. I stopped in my tracks, thinking perhaps there was an animal present, but there was nothing physical near me. The growl was captured on the audio track of my video camera.

As the evening unfolded, we split into different teams to gather evidence. Right away, we were picking up malevolent responses to our questions.

Since I was the new guy in the group, it was suggested I go to the attic for a solo session. Talk about being broken in! The attic is the spot where satanic rituals purportedly took place.

، Reluctantly I agreed and went upstairs by myself. Once in the attic, I sat down on a chair. Next to me was a creepy doll. A lot of people have a fear of dolls, but I don't personally fear them. I am aware they can be used by entities though, so I always stay aware when dolls are connected to locations.

I had an EMF meter sitting beside me and the rest of the team was watching me on a video feed. For a moment I thought about the fact that they were sitting comfortably downstairs while I was sitting in a creepy attic, beside a creepy doll waiting to see if satanic spirits were going to screw with me. It had all the makings of a horror movie, yet here I was, excited to do it.

There was complete silence in the attic for a few moments, then I heard footsteps. They were just there suddenly, and they were all around me. Along with the steps there were voices, mumbling and whispering in the darkness. I spoke out loud and said if there was someone present, they should show me a sign.

The EMF meter went off. As soon as this occurred, my shoulder turned freezing cold. Something was making its presence known. Before I could process it all, I felt a burning sensation on my back. The activity had peaked quickly then fell off. I believe the fact that I'm protected by Saint Michael is what kept me safe in the attic that night.

Later we moved out to a barn on the property. The barn itself was reportedly the site of several hangings. One investigator brought a Ouija board with him that night and he wanted me to use it. After hearing negative stories about the boards in the past, I should have known better than to toy with it, but in the heat of the moment and the excitement, I said I would try it.

I sat down in the middle of the barn with the board and asked if the sprits of any bounty hunters were present. During the years of slavery, bounty hunters would hunt down runaway slaves in the region. Some stories claimed some of the bounty hunters themselves were hung in the barn's rafters.

As we sat there working with the Ouija board, I heard what sounded like something heavy hanging from a rope and swinging back and forth. No one else present heard it but I was sure of the sound. I believe this experience was prompted by using the board and it reaffirmed my discomfort in working with the device. I would later come to believe there were other effects on me personally from toying with the Ouija.

Fortunately, we cut the session short. Most of the activity that night seemed to be in the house itself, so we returned inside to continue investigating. We turned on a sprit box to see what we could pick up. Over and over again, a voice came through naming itself *"Orobas"*

At the time, none of us had any idea what the word meant, or if it was even a name. Exhausted, we closed things up, called it a night and packed our equipment.

I slept hard after the investigation and the next morning, I woke still wondering what the word Orobas meant. A quick search on the internet brought forth the answer.

Orobas is the name of a demon.

Online dictionaries describe Orobas as a high prince of hell who commands twenty legions of demons. He is said to be able to speak with "divine essence," and knowns the past, present and future. As a deceptive entity, Orobas can grant favors. I can only imagine what the cost of such a favor would be.

Even more disturbing, when the web page pulled up with a drawing of the creature, it was depicted as a black horse standing on its hind legs, just like I had seen in my vision the night before our investigation!

Apparently, the form of a beautiful, black horse is the most favored form of this demon.

As we packed our cars and headed away from Prospect Place, I looked at the location in the rear-view mirror. What had we made contact with at this dark place? And would there be more effects to come from my time there?

The aftermath of using the Ouija board brought back my memories of an incident from my youth involving the Ouija.

When I was young, my sister and I had tried numerous times to get a Ouija board. We were fascinated by the idea but our parents, being devout Catholics, wouldn't have such at thing in the home. We managed a few times to get a board, but mom or dad would promptly throw it out.

When I was around thirteen, my sister, then sixteen, had a few friends over one night. Our parents were gone and out came a Ouija board that one of my sister's friends brought over. I watched in fascination as they began working with the board, asking questions as the planchette moved around spelling out answers.

It was hard to wrap my head around exactly what I was seeing. A weird, green energy seemed to manifest around the people working with the board. It creeped me out, but I continued to watch as things unfolded.

Something was coming through and using the board to communicate. Whatever it was told my sister that two of her close friends were going to die that year.

Suddenly, it didn't seem like a fun game anymore and everyone stopped playing.

I wish that's all there was to the story, but it's not. Later that year, my sister's best friend died in a car accident. She was only sixteen.

A little later that same year, my sister's prom date hung himself.

All of this played over again in my mind as I thought about my attempt to use a Ouija board at the goading of another investigator.

I decided then and there to stick closer to my own principles going forward and to continue to use my religious foundation when I investigated.

CHAPTER ELEVEN:
Bobby Mackey's Music World

Bobby Mackey's is one of those places that's on the bucket list of most paranormal investigators. Located in Wilder, Kentucky, it's considered the most haunted bar in America.

In its early days, the building was a slaughter house before it was turned into a roadhouse. Drinking, gambling and music were all part of the scene during the site's early days as an entertainment stop. There's also a gruesome story about a murder that took place at Bobby Mackey's.

According to the tale, a young woman named Pearl Bryan was decapitated in the area. Her body was found about two and a half miles from what was then the old slaughterhouse, but her head was never found. Legend says the murderers, Scott Jackson and Alonzo Walling, threw Pearl's head down the well on the property.

Rumors of satanism and a botched abortion have long been part of the mix in the tale of poor Pearl Bryan. Many people believe the land itself is cursed. From its years as a slaughterhouse, the land was certainly drenched in a lot of blood, and if even a few of the stories of dark rituals on the property were real, then the land could indeed be cursed.

Years after the Pearl Bryan case, there was another death on the property. A dancer name Johanna committed suicide after her father killed the man she loved. Adding to the tragedy, when Johanna killed herself, she was pregnant.

With such a mix of legends and tragic tales, I knew that Bobby Mackey's was likely going to be an intense and active location.

Meeting music legend Bobby Mackey.

Arriving at the site, we were given a brief tour of the bar. I noted the warning sign posted at the entrance. It read:

"Warning to our patrons: This establishment is purported to be haunted. Management is not responsible and cannot be held liable for any actions of any ghosts / spirits on this premises."

The place lived up to its reputation. We caught numerous EVPs that night, experienced shadow figures darting around and heard disembodied voices. We also observed what looked like eyes, peering out of the darkness and watching us. All of this was just on the main floor of the bar.

The area most known for dark energy is the basement, a place dubbed "Hell's Gate." The basement is where the opening of the well is. The same well that Pearl Bryan's head was purportedly thrown down. Some people even believe the area itself is where a satanic ritual was performed with Pearl as the sacrifice.

I entered the basement by myself and almost right away found myself drifting into a trance. I felt lost. Everything was spinning around me, and it seemed as if time had stopped. I couldn't think, I couldn't focus. I had no idea where I was or what was happening.

Suddenly I snapped out of it and came back to my senses. I couldn't remain in the basement however. I would come to believe this strange experience was a combination of the negativity of Hell's Gate and the time I had spent the previous night using a Ouija board. I left the room and returned upstairs. I hung back somewhat, trying to further access myself and remaining cautious. With the rest of the team, I continued to investigate to the early morning hours before we headed back to the hotel for some sleep.

Bobby Mackey's is also where I met Dave Spinks, a fellow investigator I would end up going on a number of trips with. Dave is passionate about the paranormal just like I am, and we would have some real adventures to come.

*　　*　　*

The paranormal road trip over, I found myself back in New York and soon realized something had changed.

I had developed a short temper. It was completely out of character for me. I would find myself overwhelmed and aggravated by the smallest incidents. Things people said, minor inconveniences all became bigger deals. I recognized it but was having a hard time shaking it off.

Other odd things started to occur too. Sitting at my computer one evening, I felt a fierce burning on the surface of my feet. I pulled the chair out and looked down to see three scratch marks on my right foot. It was bleeding. On my left foot was a bright red circular shape.

My sister happened to be going by and looked down. She was shocked and said:

"Sean, what the heck is that!? Stigmata?"

I wasn't sure what to make of the incident but slowly, other pieces of the puzzle were made clear. Two weeks later I headed out for the gym. When I got to my car, I noticed letters written on the windshield "J S."

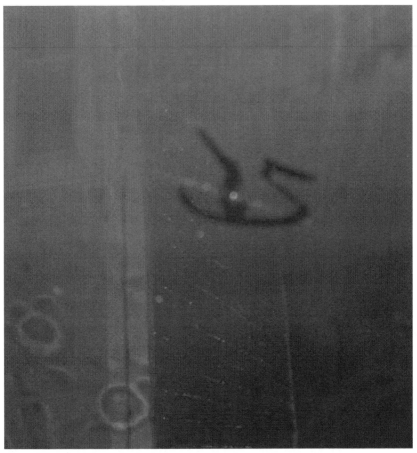

The letters "JS" appeared written on the windshield inside my car, was it the spirit of Johanna?

I would later learn that the spirit of Johanna, the dancer who died at Bobby Mackey's, was known to follow young men home. I didn't know what Johanna's last name was, or whether it started with an S, but I came to believe this was a manifestation of her spirit lingering around me. Maybe she was even trying to warn me or protect me because my personality and behavior was still going through some changes.

For a couple of months, I had been casually seeing a woman named Alyssa. It was a friendly connection, we had things in common and enjoyed hanging out, but it wasn't anything serious. At least, I didn't consider it serious at the time.

She called one day to tell me she had taken a new job and would be relocating pretty far north. I reacted with an unfamiliar feeling of intense devastation. I felt like I was saying goodbye to a dying loved one. I couldn't get my mind and my emotions balanced, I had only known her a few months, yet I felt like something was being violently ripped away.

After Alyssa moved, we tried to maintain a long-distance connection. Such things are challenging under the best of conditions and it was even more so with my changed behavior. She asked me to come up for a weekend visit at the end of August. She had invited her best friend, who was bringing her boyfriend with her, so there would be four of us. I was excited to see Alyssa and spend time with her, but I wasn't prepared for what occurred.

The weekend was a disaster. The four of us couldn't seem to get along. We were upset and fought most of the weekend, and it was all over complete nonsense. The girls were constantly crying. I felt angry and jealous, again, behavior that was out of character for me under normal conditions.

I didn't realize it at the time, but I was experiencing the early signs of oppression.

Once back home, I puzzled over the experiences from the weekend. I still had feelings for Alyssa and I wanted to repair the relationship. A few days later, she called and told me she didn't think things were going to work out between us, and that it wasn't a good idea to continue with our connection.

Again, I felt devastated. I can't begin to express how painful this was for me to go through. My whole life seemed in turmoil and I couldn't pull myself together. I started waking up at five am and would pace up and down the stairs. I was in pain that was emotional, mental and physical. I thought about how to end things because the pain was so bad. I'd never had such thoughts in my life, never thought about harming myself, yet now the thoughts pushed into my mind constantly.

At work, I'd frequently go to the bathroom just to splash cold water on my face, trying to snap out of the strange despondent state I was in.

Waves of spiritual pain came over me and at times I felt like a puppet, completely at the mercy of something beyond me. Sometimes while driving, one of these waves would hit and I would have to pull over until it passed, and I could safely control myself enough to get home.

I continued trying to go through the motions of my life. I found myself at a cemetery one night trying to do an investigation, searching for something to pull me out and make me feel alive. A smell I can only describe as rotting flesh came out of nowhere and I fell into a trance like the one I had experienced in the basement at Bobby Mackey's.

As this was happening, my recorder was rolling, and I captured a disturbing EVP. The creepy voice said:

"Hail Satan. Hail Beelzebub."

I got in my car and rushed home. The EVP had shaken me up, but it may have been what I needed in a sense. I started researching psychic protection and found an exercise used to ground the emotions. Inspired, and desperate to try anything, I gave the brief ritual a try.

I stood up and imagined roots flowing out of my feet and deep into the ground. I took deep breathes through my nose and exhaled through my mouth. All while I imagined white light flowing through my body. I was visualizing negativity leaving my body and as I went through the process, I spoke out loud:

"I am grounded, and I am of this Earth, surrounded by the white light of Jesus Christ. With his light, I am protected and safe from harm."

I stood there and repeated the process several times. When I was done, I felt seventy-five percent better. I opened my eyes and saw a big ball of glowing, red energy flying away from me and out of the window. I was astonished and cussed out loud. I was angry with the realization that something very negative had been attached to me and had been feeding on the darkness that had been surrounding me.

I realized in that moment that I had been suffering under demonic oppression.

Despite my regular prayers of protection, something, somehow had gotten through. My mind went back to the investigations I had conducted at Bobby Mackey's, and what I believed to be the presence of Johanna. Maybe this oppression was the same thing she had suffered, causing her to take her own life and that of her unborn child.

I had never contemplated suicide, and under normal conditions, I can't for a moment imagine coming to a place where things were so bad that I would take my own life. But after suffering this period of oppression, I believe I have a new understanding of how that can happen to some people and how the darkness can become so intense that there seems to be no other escape from it.

Looking back further on what led to my experience, I came to believe it was my brief time spent using the Ouija board at Prospect Place. Although I was pressured to work with it, I knew I had to bear the responsibility myself for using it and opening a door for something negative to enter my life. Perhaps my vision right before the investigation, the vision of the demonic horse rearing up, was a warning that I didn't understand at the time. Something dark had taken hold and manipulated my mind and emotions.

Ultimately, I came out on the other side stronger and better, with a deeper understanding and a new set of tools to defend against the darkness. I had endured and there was more work to be done.

CHAPTER TWELVE:
The Sterling Opera House

After going through the period of oppression, I wrote a flood of songs. Perhaps it was the profound emotional experience I had been through, maybe it was the renewed attitude that gave me a burst of creative energy.

Either way, the music flowed. From the time I was young, music was a vital part of my life. I always referred to music as my "invisible therapist." Growing up, I found that I would at times isolate myself, distancing myself from other people at home and school, and losing myself in music.

It helped me through a lot of emotional trials growing up, and it's one of the things that lead me to become a songwriter. When I began to be more conscious of my spiritual self, I began to appreciate music on an even deeper level.

I think that music goes well beyond the physical plane and connects with our souls. Sometimes my music is channeled from somewhere so deep I feel a part of my soul energy is in the music. At times I've written lyrics in a flurry of energy and afterwards, I'm puzzled by the words and the layers of their meanings.

For me, every song triggers some specific emotion; love, anger, happiness, sadness, the whole range of human experience comes alive in music.

There's nothing more empowering than writing a song that has an impact on the listeners. Music can change lives, offer strength and comfort and even guidance. Ultimately, it molded me into the person I am today. Music and spirituality have become my right and left hands, they are two passions that I could never give up.

My next investigation had a connection to music and it was one I was really looking forward to.

*   *   *

The Sterling Opera House in Derby, Connecticut was built in 1889. Over its long history, a wide range of entertainers graced its stage from music acts to plays and other types of live theatre.

The once beautiful building had been sitting empty and abandoned for almost fifty years, and there were a range of paranormal reports about the place. A local art gallery owner named Rich had access to the place and permitted us to investigate.

Rich led us into the building and gave us a tour. Along the way, he told us about the different types of activity reported at the Opera House. Shadow figures, balls of light and a little child that liked to play with a ball were all part of the tales associated with the location.

The stage was large and had three tiers. Rich pointed out Harry Houdini's trapdoor, still there in the middle of the stage. I was fascinated at the history it held. So many legendary performers had been here.

Under the stage was another world. The bottom floor of the building had once been city hall. There were also remnants of several jail cells. Rich told us that one cell at the back end was where a prisoner named Marc Carbone was kept. Carbone had allegedly murdered someone with an icepick, a brutal crime. I stepped into the cell for a moment and the vibe inside was eerie and uncomfortable.

A ball of energy at Sterling Opera House.

I had several friends with me for this investigation. Phil, Glen, Amy and a couple of others that had tagged along. It was a big location and it was my first time inside.

Glenn had never experienced anything paranormal, but he tagged along anyway. A lot of people are curious and open to see if they'll have anything happen at haunted locations.

We were doing an EVP session and heard some weird, disembodied voices whispering to us. It's an old building, so we were objective about the various sounds we were hearing and picking up on recordings. Still, it was curious that there were things happening already.

Since there were so many stories about a little boy playing with a ball, we tried an experiment. We sat a ball in front of us so that it was completely still, then we asked the little boy, who people call Andy, to move the ball. Moments later, the ball moved and started rolling down the stairs.

Later that evening, we headed to the bottom floor to check out the old city hall and the jail cells. We split up with a couple of us in each of the jail cells, and started asking the spirits to make their presence known.

Unfortunately, things took a different turn at this point. My friend Amy had brought her boyfriend with her. I hadn't met him before and certainly had no idea of how he would start behaving. Sitting in one of the cells, he started to shout at the spirits, challenging whatever was there to do something. He kept saying that it couldn't do anything to us and he taunted over and over. As this was happening, Glenn felt a wave of dread come over him. He seemed confused and asked what was going on.

A loud banging noise started in one of the cells, we all jumped up and looked at each other wondering if someone in our group had made the sound. No one had. The banging happened two more times. Amy, who was sitting in the cell with her boyfriend while he taunted, reported pains in her lower back. She jumped up and lifted the back of her shirt, telling us it was painful. We quickly saw that she had been scratched, but it wasn't just a surface mark, this scratch was an open wound.

We decided it was best to leave the jail cells and head back to the main floor. Amy and Glenn were both ready to get out of there that night but the rest of us wanted to do a little more.

I stepped over to an area myself and asked the spirits if they could float a ball of energy right over my hand as I raised it up towards the ceiling. Phil had his camera out and snapped a series of three pictures of me while I was speaking. In the first two photos, everything is normal, but in the third pic, three perfect spheres of light can be seen floating above my raised hand. I was convinced the manifestation was not the result of dust. The odds of the placement and the timing were undeniable evidence of spiritual energy responding to my request.

Glenn took a look at the photos and made a comment about them being surreal. He told us he'd had enough and was going outside to wait for us in the car.

We investigated a little while longer. At one point, we heard what sounded like doors shaking hard. We couldn't place where the sound came from and we wondered if someone was outside, trying to get into the opera house.

Once we were finished, we met up with Glenn who was waiting in the car. He told us that while he was sitting there, he had observed the front doors suddenly shake violently. The doors were locked and couldn't be opened without a key. Curiously, Rich told us police officers had been called to the location intermittently because the front doors were discovered standing open. I was left wondering if something was trying to get in or out.

There's a postscript to this investigation. Amy's cut plagued her for some time. She later told me:

"Once we got home, I went to bed. I noticed a shadow at the end of my bed. It was a dark mass, not a specific shape. I turned on the lights and discovered two red scratch marks on my wrist. About a week later, my back still had not started to heal. It wouldn't scab, it just remained an open cut. I went to the dermatologist and the doctor told me that an infection might be starting, so I was prescribed antibiotic cream to put on it, along with Neosporin once I was done with the cream. It took almost a month for the marks to begin to scab, and then almost another month for it to finally heal. To this day a scar remains. I never would have believed this if it wasn't on me. It wasn't just a 'scratch.' There was a cut, almost a gouge mark."

Was it the spirit of the icepick killer, angered at the taunting going on in the jail cells? We can never be sure, but for me, the Sterling Opera House was an amazing investigation and the experiences were unforgettable.

CHAPTER THIRTEEN:
Letchworth Village Asylum

In the town of Thiells, Rockland County, New York, there's a sprawling, abandoned institution. Opened in 1911, the site was originally built for the physically and mentally disabled.

During its most active period, Letchworth Village consisted of more than 130 buildings on a property of several acres.

In 1950, the first trial of the polio vaccine was administered at Letchworth, given to an eight-year-old patient. When there were no side effects, the vaccine was given to another nineteen subjects. It proved successful in seventeen of the cases.

The site was named after William Pryor Letchworth, a man dedicated to the treatment, reform and care of the mentally ill. Sadly, as with many such sites, rumors of abuse, rape and horrible conditions arose. Poor funding plagued the facility for a long time, but somehow it managed to remain open until 1996 when it finally shut its doors.

Letchworth now sits abandoned, stained with the memory of years of reports of negative events. A recipe for paranormal activity if ever there was one.

Gregory and I ventured to Letchworth one night to see what kind of evidence we could find. There were plenty of stories of hauntings at the site, no surprise with the wide-ranging reports of abuse that had taken place. There was even talk of rogue science experiments at the site, experiments on the human brain and other monstrous things.

With Gregory at Letchworth Asylum.

A few miles down the road from Letchworth is a cemetery, filled with the deceased that came out of the asylum. Only numbers differentiate the graves. In days long past, many people were abandoned by their families, left to die at the asylum and be buried with no one to mourn them. Some stories claim there are several bodies in each grave.

We scouted the area well to see what we could easily get access to. We had to wear masks due to the asbestos in the buildings.

We located the main building and went inside. It was an

eerie sight. In every room, it looked like the staff had suddenly stopped what they were doing, dropped everything and fled. Remnants of the institution were everywhere. Patient records, drawings, implements, furnishings and more. We found dental records and x-rays, mouthpieces, dishes, it was all such a strange thing to see.

We explored all the way up to the third floor of the main building and then entered a smaller adjacent building. It looked like a dormitory, probably rooms for the patients who had lived on the site.

We heard loud, reverberating footsteps echo through the building, but we were sure no one else was there.

After getting a good sense of the layout of the buildings in the daylight, we left the village with a plan to return for a nighttime investigation.

When we returned to Letchworth, it was in the pitch black. It was so dark, we almost ran face first into a building! We carefully found our point of entry and made our way into the main structure.

Making our way through the building, we heard some strange sounds. We weren't sure what to make of them, so we pressed on.

We made our way downstairs to the basement were the morgue had been located. I was filming with my cell phone's camera and caught an odd mist forming in front of us. There was no draft and the mist appeared to have a life of its own. It moved towards us then pulled back and disappeared. I yelled over to Gregory telling him what I had just caught on camera.

Once we started exploring the morgue, we discovered what appeared to be an experimental laboratory right next to the morgue. Supposedly the brains of patients were once kept in canisters in the room.

We stepped into the laboratory to do a spirit box session, then suddenly heard some chatter from elsewhere in the building. It got louder and was approaching us. Sadly, it was nothing paranormal. A group of young kids were wandering around in the halls. Standing there wearing my breathing mask, I was tempted to give them a good scare but decided against it. I had to give in to the temptation when we heard what the kids were talking about, though. One of them was mouthing off about there being nothing scary in the building, no such things as ghost and so forth. By coincidence, Gregory and I looked a bit like doctors with our breathing masks on. Those kids walked straight into the laboratory and the moment they did, Gregory turned on our laser grid and I let out a loud screeching noise.

The kids were ass over elbow running out of the building and screaming about getting out of there and not coming back. We could hear them as they left the building and continued running down the street.

We went to a window and watched as their flashlights jerked all over the place on their flight out of the asylum. Gregory and I could hardly stop laughing. I thought to myself, those kids will probably tell their grandkids this ghost story someday.

I may have felt bad briefly for giving those kids such a scare, but there's another aspect to it too. Letchworth has suffered a lot of vandalism over the years. Sadly, the site has been abandoned so long and no one has the funds to do anything with it, that the site, and the spirits there, are left to continue suffering.

At least, I thought, that's one group of kids that won't be breaking things or spray painting on walls!

Comic relief over, we cleared our heads and got back to the investigation at hand. We turned on the spirit box and received some creepy responses to our questions. The box started saying *"bad demon"* over and over. It was as if the spirits in the place were trying to warn us something bad was in the room with us.

We decided to move our investigation to another part of the building and go all the way to the third floor. As we were climbing the stairs, we continued to hear strange noises. We still weren't sure if they were normal noises produced by the aged structure, or if something unseen was attempting to make its presence known.

As we were moving through the building, both of our

flashlights started to dim. At that moment, we heard a deep male voice making a long groaning sound. The moan was horrible, like someone in terrible pain. With the combination of that sound, and our now dead flashlights, we decided to leave and return another night. We were pretty creeped out between the sounds and the lack of light, and making it back to the car in pitch black was a real challenge and a bit dangerous.

The next day, we did some further research on the location. We discovered that other investigators had experienced the moaning noises on the third floor, so it was another confirmation for us.

Another friend of mine was interested in doing some investigating. Phil Arnone joined Gregory and I one evening for another excursion to Letchworth Village. It was Good Friday.

We went back to the laboratory area and Phil and I both had a sensation as if something had passed through us. We became a little dizzy and light-headed. I had felt such things before, but it was a new experience for Phil. He laughed nervously and said, "That might be enough for my first time."

I told him to keep calm and take some deep breaths. "We'll just make our way through the building."

By the time we reached the third floor, we heard the same painful moaning voice Gregory and I had heard before. About five feet away, a door slowly creaked open while we all stood there watching in silence. When it was almost fully open, the door slammed itself shut. This happened three times in a row.

Phil grabbed us both by the arms and said:

"All right guys, this is really enough for my first time!"

I was creeped out like the other guys, but I wanted to make sure there was no logical reason for the door's movement, so I walked over to it and kicked it. The door was so heavy it barely moved. There was no wind coming in the building anyway, but the weight of the door added to the puzzle of how it could have moved in such a way.

The whole experience really rattled Phil, but at the same time, it piqued his interest enough that he wanted to join in on other investigations.

I've investigated Letchworth on many occasions. It's one of the locations that I've found myself very drawn to. On one outing, a voice on the spirit box started saying *"Evil doctor!"* During these responses, we heard what sounded like a girl screaming in the hallway adjacent to us. I started to feel as if some of the spirits at Letchworth were trapped there by a negative entity.

I started saying prayers for the souls that were there, directing them to go to the light and to God, and calling on the name of Jesus.

The responses from the spirit box reached a new level of nastiness. Threats started spewing out and we heard a deafening banging sound on a pipe in the building.

I wasn't trying to agitate negative entities. I merely wanted to help any souls who wanted to move on. The energy was getting very intense and we decided it best to leave.

Leaving Letchworth Village, there's a path that leads to the road near the woods. Just as we reached the end of the path that day, a large, heavy rock landed about ten feet away from us. It was so heavy that we felt the vibration in the ground when it hit.

There was no other movement in the woods around us. We rushed back to the car. I put holy water all around the car and said a prayer asking that nothing follow us from the site. Right after the prayer, there was another loud bang like something hit the roof of my car. Again, there was no one around and no clear source of these things being thrown at us. I believe it was an evil entity, angered that I was trying to help souls in the Asylum cross over.

I've taken so many trips to Letchworth at this point, that it would take an entire book to cover all the details of the investigations. What follows are some of the highlights that I've experienced there.

Phil and I returned another night with our friends Amy and Christy in tow. We were up on the third floor again and I asked the spirits if they could move the door as they had done previously. This time, the activity occurred at a different door. One of the rooms had a metal chair holding open its door. The chair shook violently after my request. We all stepped back in unison thinking someone had entered the room. There was nothing there. I walked over to the chair and moved it myself, perfectly replicating the sound we had just heard.

We entered the room where the chair was propping the door open. Once inside, I started getting a strong impression of someone practicing witchcraft. Shining my flashlight towards the floor, I noticed there were burn marks there. I held my hand out over the area. It was bitter cold that night, but I could feel heat rising from the spot. Next, we all noticed an inexplicable stench around us. It smelled like farm animals. It was thick and potent and just as quickly as it arrived, it was gone.

We turned on the spirit box and it started making references to satanic activity. I received a clairvoyant flash of an evil, grinning face. I looked over at Amy and saw that she didn't look right. She was staring off into nowhere. I asked her again if she was alright and she said half her body was on fire. She said she felt a burning sensation on her back and when we looked, we discovered three scratches on her back.

Christy chimed in and said she felt nauseous. Feeling concerned for the two girls, I motioned that we should leave the room. Once outside, I put holy water on their foreheads and gave them a prayer to repeat.

As we were leaving the site that night, we heard what sounded like furniture being thrown about in a violent manner.

A week after this trip, Amy called and reported that she experienced the farm animal stench in her bedroom one night. Even her father had noticed the smell and came to ask her where the awful odor was coming from. I gave her some prayers to recite and the manifestation went away.

Despite my regular protective prayers, things do still happen to me. Negative entities feed off fear, so it's important to stay strong in your faith. They are always looking for openings to attack.

On another occasion, Phil and I and another friend were in the same dormitory room using a spirit box. I made a comment that I hoped my prayers had helped some of the souls at the site.

A female voice came through the box and a wave of emotion hit me at the same time. I had never experienced anything like it before. It was a sense of helplessness, as if life was over. There was no hope. I started having flashes of a girl slitting her wrists and ending her life. The sensations were incapacitating.

The guys were asking me if I was alright, and I was able to snap out of the vision. I understood the girl's spirit had projected her emotions on to me and I experienced the things she did in the last moments of her life.

I repeated my hope that prayers could help some of the souls at Letchworth find peace. A long growl came out of the spirit box. It was loud as a dinosaur! Clearly, something wasn't happy with my attempts at helping spirits seek forgiveness.

At home that night, I was visited by an evil spirit in the form of a pale humanoid with white, glowing eyes. It was bald and had no shirt on. A pentagram was burned in the middle of its forehead. It tried to choke me in my sleep and I again suffered sleep paralysis.

Letchworth has a long history and many dark things happened there. It seems the struggle that many of the people suffered while living has continued in the afterlife.

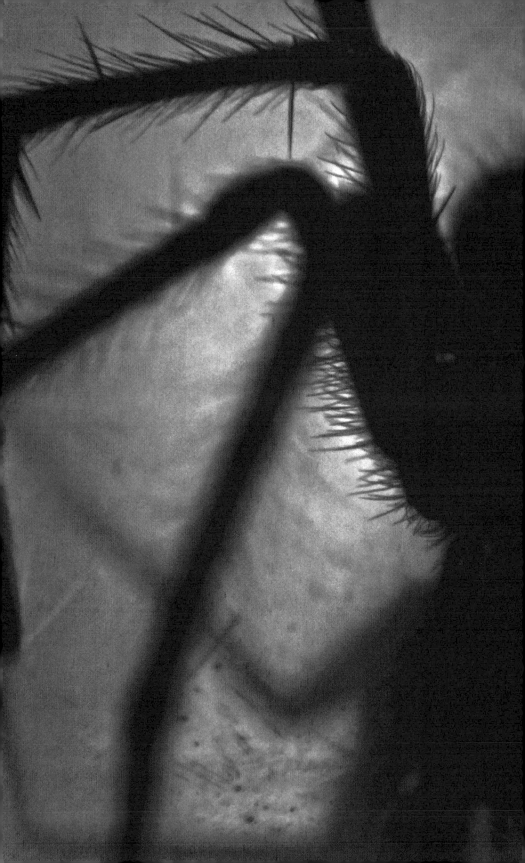

CHAPTER FOURTEEN:
Out of Body and into the Astral

In a lucid dream, you're conscious that you're dreaming, and you can direct your own actions. It's a state that many people experience on occasion. I had a strong, lucid experience one night that I bounced up and out of my physical body. I hovered there for a moment then thought about going through the roof and down the street. In a second, I was flying over the neighborhood.

The view of the houses was vivid, and I rose up to the sky then came back down and landed. People were walking all around. I was escorted into a building and sat down in an office.

A gentleman sitting behind the desk started explaining astral projection to me. Somehow, I knew my grandfather was sitting beside me and that he was wearing his army fatigues, though I never turned to look at him.

I woke up remembering the details of the flight and the conversation and it stuck with me.

For years, people have talked about leaving their bodies during sleep or meditation. I had never tried to do it myself but had frequently had very lucid dream experiences.

For me, the experiences came at random, so I decided to do some research on the topic. I found a book called "Astral

Voyages," by Bruce Goldberg. In the book, Goldberg shares specific experiences of delving into the astral plane. He talks about the astral plane where ghosts exist, and the lower realms inhabited by negative and demonic entities. He also mentions higher levels of the astral plane where lighter vibrations exist, and the frequency is higher. Each level moving up is one step closer to God.

The book also discusses reincarnation and the idea that each life is a chance to learn the lessons needed to brighten the soul and improve the higher self, thus, graduating to another level of existence on the astral planes.

Being raised Catholic, the information was new for me, but it resonated with my sense of things and helped put more of the pieces together for me spiritually. While my core belief will always be that of the Catholic faith, I have always tried to remain open to other spiritual ideas that can further my understanding of the whole of our lives.

In the course of my research, I also learned about the Akashic records.

The Akashic records are supposed to be a kind of spiritual library containing information on everything that has passed and everything that is to come. It's believed that psychics access the Akashic records when they do readings and retrieve information for individuals.

As I was leaning more about the astral plane, out of body experiences, and the Akashic records, I continued having experiences. I wanted to try some test to see what I could do and experience, so I asked my friend Phil to go to his room and write down a random word on a piece of paper and leave it sitting in plain view.

The next time I left my body in a lucid state, I activated my thoughts to carry me to Phil's house. I travelled quickly and found myself landing in Phil's bedroom. I looked around and spotted a note. When I walked over and looked at it, I couldn't quite focus on what was written, the words seemed blurry and weren't legible. (I later learned that reading while astral projecting is extremely difficult)

As I was standing in Phil's room, I heard a noise and turned to look over at him. Phil was fast asleep, but he was talking in his sleep. I listened for a moment and he was talking about EVPs. I stood there for a moment laughing, for some reason I found the moment hysterical.

The next morning, I woke with full memory of my excursion that night. I called Phil and told him what had happened, and that I'd heard him talking in his sleep about EVPs.

"That's weird." He replied. "My brother caught me doing that a week ago, and also thought it was pretty damn funny."

*　　*　　*

Other lucid experiences were of a much more serious nature and there were a series of visions I had that I believe related to the times of Jesus and before.

In one, I found myself watching a scene unfold. There were two huge mountains in the background with the sun shining between them. There was a large field before me. On the left were thousands of beautiful, white angels. On the right, there was a hill, and on top of it there were thousands of dark creatures. The angels and the dark creatures ran towards each other.

It looked like the start of a spiritual war.

The angels bore swords and shields and the two forces went at each other viciously.

One angel then turned towards me, looked me in the eyes and said:

"Sean, you have to remember who you are. Remember!"

The vision shifted. There was a sword in the dirt. I was on a cliff overlooking the fields below the mountains. There was a man and a woman, they were wearing togas and holding a baby in front of thousands of people. There were white pillars everywhere.

A voice cried out:

"Behold! The King of Argos!"

On other occasions, I would see Jesus there in my visions. Once I saw him explaining to a group of men why he had to be crucified and how it was meant to happen. There was so much emotional energy in the experience it was almost overwhelming.

On another journey, I saw myself as a young boy in church with my father. I heard a very calm voice state:

"Sean, you're really going back too far. You need to come back."

I felt a big pull and I woke up humming church music.

After each experience, I would lay there and think about what I had seen and felt, trying to make sense of the visions. I believe I was traveling back in time, sometimes on the thread of my own life, but other times, much farther back where I witnessed real events that occurred in the past.

Over time, I learned to tell the difference between "normal" dreams and these visionary experiences. They have a different quality to them and a richness that is beyond that of a regular dream.

Another experience was frightening. I had just dozed off when I felt someone, or something, grab me around the neck. I felt my astral body being pulled out of my physical body.

I was falling off a tall building, down, down, I landed in a dark tunnel. Everything around me was black, pitch black and for a moment I couldn't see anything but darkness. As dark as it was, I saw something moving. It was even darker than the pitch blackness around me. It was crawling out of the darkness like a spider. It crawled from side to side and then to the top of the tunnel. It was heading straight towards me.

I looked down at my hands. Both of my palms were glowing with white fire. As the spider creature came quickly towards me, I put my arms forward and a white, glowing fire shot from both of my palms and towards the horrible creature.

The fire looked like it was filled with small, shiny crystals. I could hear the creature snarling and screeching as it headed towards me, but when the light from my hands went forth, it quickly turned and scurried away.

I woke up in a sweat, shaking off the sleep paralysis I had been in yet again. I knew that the experience had been real, and I quickly said some prayers of protection.

Leaving the body and astral projecting is both exciting and a bit frightening, and it's important to always take measures to be protected. The light that shone from my hands was, for me, another confirmation of my belief we are all part of the light, and as God's children, we are all capable of projecting the light from within us.

CHAPTER FIFTEEN:
Investigating Historic Ohio

John Farnam was a special agent for General George Washington during the American Revolution. As one of only eight survivors from the battle of Monmouth, he was considered a war hero. He married Mary Everett, and together, the couple had nine children.

At the end of the war, Farnam was given the opportunity to purchase 1,200 acres of land in what is now known as Furnace Run Valley in East Richfield, Ohio. In 1812, Farnam moved his wife and seven of their children to the new homestead. In time, the Farnam family built what is now known as Farnam Manor.

In November 2015, Dave Spinks asked me if I'd join him on some investigations in Ohio, including the historic Farnam Manor. I didn't hesitate to answer yes. Although I didn't know much about the location, I did know it had a reputation for being very haunted and I was eager to check it out.

When we arrived at the site, I could feel the energy right away. My body reacts to locations that are haunted, and I knew this was going to be a good investigation.

The couple who own the manor were very gracious and gave us a tour of the house and grounds. With an obvious love of history and preservation, they pointed out many interesting facts about the breathtaking manor house.

With Dave Spinks at Farnam Manor.

Even during the tour, I was picking up on spiritual energy in the home. In one room, I saw a big ball of dark orange spirit energy. The room felt very active. Nothing at Farnam felt negative, there was just a lot of energy all around the manor.

Once the owners left, we started setting up our equipment for the night's investigation. We were in the kitchen getting cameras ready when we heard what sounded like heavy boot steps walking above us. The house was empty except for us, but I ran upstairs just to check if anyone was there. There was nothing, no physical person in any of the rooms over us, nor anywhere else in the house. What a start to the night!

As the investigation unfolded, we received numerous intelligent responses on spirit boxes and via EVP. We also heard the chatter of little children and caught the sound on some of our recordings.

Dave was using a FLIR camera and pointed it at the grounds outside the room we were in. An amazing image was captured as something moved across the lawn just outside. There was no other living person on the property with us!

Later, while sitting at the large dining room table, Dave was running the FLIR again and had it pointed down a nearby hallway. Again, we captured another amazing piece of evidence as a human shaped torso suddenly leaned in from around the corner at the end of the hallway. Something unseen was taking a peek at us to see what we were doing.

Our second night in Farnam Manor was just as active as the first. We experienced more phantom footsteps, a wide range of banging and tapping noises from around the house, and more disembodied voices.

At one point, we were investigating in a room with a large fireplace. I was sitting on a couch, about fifteen feet from the fire and I was in deep thought. Often, in haunted locations, I find myself worried over the idea that there could be souls who are lost or trapped at the location. I was thinking about this very topic that night and I had the inspiration to say a prayer for any spirits that needed to find peace, be they from the manor itself, or spirits simply attracted to my energy.

Just as I was about to pray, a male voice screamed over the spirit box we had running. *"Come over here!"* it shouted.

Was something trying to get my attention or trying to frighten me? I walked over to the fireplace and made a statement of my faith. Afterwards, I started saying a prayer for the release of any spirits around me that were trapped or in need of help.

I felt a sense of calm and focused on white light coming down to guide any spirits in need. As I was visualizing this, I had a vision flash in my mind of a beautiful white dove.

At that moment, a female voice on the spirit box said, *"Thank you."*

In seconds another distinctly different female voice also said thank you.

The voices came from two separate boxes we had running.

It was a great feeling and another confirmation for me of the power of prayer and its ability to offer comfort even to those not in physical form.

In time, the symbol of a white dove in flight would come to represent female spirits for me. Male spirits, in my mind's eye, would be represented by a white horse.

*   *   *

While Dave Spinks and I were in Ohio, we also investigated another haunted location that for privacy reasons must remain undisclosed. Unlike the peacefulness of Farnam Manor, this location seemed to have a more negative influence. At one time, the house had been a brothel and there were rumors that abortions and abuse had occurred on the site.

We were spending two nights at the location and as soon as Dave and I walked in, we both felt a wave of energy hit us. It struck me like a ton of bricks and whatever it was, it felt very negative to me. The house had a basement, and we were drawn to go down the stairs and explore it briefly as we were getting the lay of the house. Going down the stairs, we both felt our equilibrium was off. It became difficult to walk and we couldn't even keep ourselves straight. It sunk in that this would be our home for the next two nights.

During our first session with a spirit box, a ball of energy flew towards the box, hovered and swung back and forth over the speaker, then took off!

I was having unsettling visions while staying in the house, and many of the voices we received on the spirit box were negative in nature. There was even the sound of a woman screaming at one point.

If the house had truly been used for abortions in the distant past, it could explain some of the dark and heavy energy I was picking up.

The following day, the home owner's son told us about an incident that had happened to him in the home. One day, he received a telephone call. The caller did not identify themselves, nor did he recognize the voice. The caller stated:

"You need to come down to the basement."

The call ended. Worried that something was wrong, the man rushed to the home and went directly to the basement. There was no one anywhere in the house. He started to feel very worried standing in the vacant home, so he left immediately.

With Gregory at Letchworth Asylum.

On our second night of investigating the historic house we continued to experience a range of anomalous sounds, loud banging noises on the ceiling, and nasty responses on the ghost box. Before going to bed, I placed holy water in the four corners of the room for protection and to help me get a good night's sleep. It had been a long week and I was exhausted.

I said some additional prayers of protection and placed my rosary in a perfect circle to my left.

The next morning when I rose, I found my rosary had been moved and was now at the bottom far corner of the bed, the farthest from me, in a messy pile. I knew there was no way I had moved the rosary in my sleep.

It was our third day in the house, and my friend Jackie was stopping by to investigate with us that night. Jackie was working on a movie nearby and it was great to have her join us, especially since this would now add a female to the mix in a location where women had purportedly been treated poorly. Perhaps she would instigate some different interactions with whatever spirits were in the home.

We were investigating in the basement when Jackie said she felt a burning sensation on her neck. Dave and I quickly checked and sure enough, there was a huge, red scratch mark on her neck. As we stood there looking at the scratch, it turned into a bright, red welt. After that, things intensified. Jackie bent over and told us pains had erupted in her female areas.

Was she empathically picking up on the illegal abortions that were performed on the site? We wasted no time escorting her off the property for her own safety. We recited a prayer over her, put holy water on her and waited to make sure she was recovered. Once she was feeling better, she went on her way, leaving us at the house by ourselves again.

I went back into the house and walked around, sprinkling holy water everywhere while saying a prayer and calling on the authority of Jesus Christ of Nazareth.

There were repercussions from this investigation that stayed with me. At one point, we were receiving communication from one of the spirit boxes from a male voice claiming to be a doctor. Whatever or whoever it was, it had a nasty attitude and directed its anger at me.

"You took two women from me."

I replied that if he was a lost spirit, he should accept what he had done wrong, accept unconditional love and God's forgiveness, and move on to the light.

"I will in time" was the response we received.

We closed our investigation down and Dave headed back home. Having friends to visit in the area, I decided to stay and got a hotel in a nearby town. That night I had a disturbing vision.

I saw a sinister face. It was red in color and looked like a devil, black horns protruded from the forehead, it had fangs shining from its open mouth and its eyes were yellow and glowing. I felt like the thing was staring into my soul.

I heard a deep-toned voice speak, saying: *"There are rules."*

There were other faces too, one was a zombie-like humanoid thing with black eyes, or no eyes, just empty black sockets. It was moving its index finger across its neck in a threatening manner while looking directly at me. In a nasty voice it said,

"You're dead."

After the trip was over, I discovered odd red marks on both of my wrists and the tops of my feet. They were rectangular in shape and I believe it was some kind of reflection of the work I had been doing. The spirit of the doctor still follows me to this day. Occasionally he will try to project negative energies towards me or induce nightmares. When he does, I again invoke my spiritual protections and continue to offer him the opportunity to go to the light and seek God. Perhaps one day he'll take me up on the suggestion.

Black horns protruded from the forehead.
(Illustration by Kimberly Carper).

"There are rules." (Illustration by Kimberly Carper).

CHAPTER SIXTEEN:
A Musical & Haunted Birthday

It was February of 2016 and my birthday was quickly approaching. I wanted to have a paranormal adventure to celebrate and the perfect opportunity arose.

I had become friends with a guy named Kevin Strahle who's better known as the YouTube star "LA Beast." Beast is a "competitive eater" and had made a name for himself by doing outrageous things on livestream. Obviously, this mostly consisted of eating things that would make other people sick. Some of his videos featured stunts like eating a full cactus, thorns and all, chugging a hundred raw eggs and eating a five-pound bag of gummy bears.

Beast wanted to go on a ghost hunt and asked me if I would join him. We arranged an event at the notorious Bobby Mackey's in Kentucky. My friend Phil would be joining us, as would Dave Spinks.

It was blistering cold that night—single digits and below zero with the wind chill, so we tried to prepare for the worst. We set up for our investigation on the main floor of the bar and in no time at all, we were catching evidence.

Several of us saw a distinct shadow figure dart across the room.

At Bobby Mackey's with L.A. Beast.

There were also strange knocking noises coming from the walls around us. We tried to explain this but could find no rational explanation to debunk it.

Inside the location was so cold we had to spend periods out in the vehicle with the heat running just to warm up.

After some time on the main floor, we moved the investigation upstairs to the apartment over the bar. At one time, the bar's caretaker/maintenance man, Carl Lawson, had lived there.

For many years, Carl was a vital part of Bobby Mackey's. He became very familiar with the spirits that reside there and he suffered a series of attacks at the hands of some unseen, negative force. In fact, after being attacked by dark entities, Carl claimed he was possessed by two demonic entities that resided in the bowels of Bobby Mackey's. Carl was given an exorcism. The ritual was filmed, and video of Carl's exorcism can still be found online. It's an eerie piece of footage to watch.

The minister performing the exorcism confirmed Carl's belief that he was possessed and was able to cast out the demons. But reports are that Carl was never quite the same after the exorcism.

Carl passed away in 2012 and since that time, numerous people have claimed to have received messages from him while at Bobby Mackey's. Was his spirit still at the location? We decided to try to find our own answer and, once in the apartment, we started an EVP session with the question:

"Carl are you still here?"

The answer came in clear and quick:

"Yes, I am here with you."

Sometimes people become so attached to locations that even after death, their spirit remains. Apparently, this is the case with Carl.

We continued to get EVPs while in the apartment and most of them seemed to be direct communication from Carl.

Dave asked a question about the well:

"Is the basement really a portal to hell?"

"Yes," came the crystal-clear response.

At that moment we all felt the floor of the apartment shake. Again, we could find no logical explanation.

The next segment of our investigation was conducted in the basement, the area known as the "portal to hell."

We set up in the basement near the well and began doing a ghost box session. While doing this, we also conducted what is called a "flashlight session."

A flashlight is placed where no one can touch it and the spirits are asked to manipulate the light, causing it to turn off and on in response to questions.

As we were conducting these sessions, we heard a loud bang and something bouncing in the room ahead of us.

Puzzled over the noise, we turned on flashlights and did a search. We discovered a metal chewing tobacco container on the floor. The container had been sitting on a table fifteen feet on the other side of the room. Something had thrown the container over our heads and to the other side of the room from where it originally sat!

Physical manipulation of objects is always a stunning event at haunted locations.

Exhausted and still freezing, we closed the investigation down and headed to the hotel to defrost.

The following night, we were special guests for the LA Beast livestream. It was a graphic eating display that I'd just as soon forget. The night wrapped up with performances by Bobby Mackey who even invited me on stage to perform "Last Kiss." It was a great moment for me and one I'll always remember.

We also had a chance to speak with Bobby and his wife who graciously listened to our recordings from Carl's apartment. Bobby confirmed there was no mistake—the voice we captured was indeed that of his departed friend Carl.

CHAPTER SEVENTEEN:
Sedamsville Rectory

After the events at Bobby Mackey's, I had another visionary experience. I had fallen asleep in bed and three children approached me and started tugging at my arms.

They kept warning me about a demon and as they tugged at my arms, items in the room around us began to levitate. There were loud bangs issuing from somewhere in the room. I noticed another person in the room and realized it was my friend Phil. We both felt confused about what was going on and we both had a sense of fear.

I was drawn to a window and walked over to look outside. I saw a large, black donkey with red eyes. It was hee-hawing over and over while running in circles around the house. I looked around more as I was watching the donkey. To the left of the front yard, there was a huge, black peacock, it too had red eyes and it was making loud screeching noises.

I sprang awake, chilled to the bone.

The next morning, I called Phil and told him what I dreamt. I was surprised to learn that he'd had a similar dream the night before. I didn't know what all the symbols meant, but I knew that I would need to be very guarded going into the next location on my trip.

With our time at Bobby Mackey's being wrapped up, we went over the border to Ohio to check out Sedamsville Rectory.

The Rectory has long had a reputation for paranormal activity. The location is a bit of a puzzle because there's nothing in terms of historical information to explain why there's activity going on. There are however, a lot of various rumors of dark things having occurred in the building. A lot of people believe that child molestation took place in the Rectory. At some point after it was closed, there were illegal dog fights conducted at the site too.

The weather was still freezing cold on the day we first walked into Sedamsville Rectory. As I walked around getting a feel for the energy, I recognized one of the rooms as the same one I was standing in during my dream the previous night.

I found the basement of the Rectory a very unsettling place. While down there, I heard the whining of dogs and had visions of the terrible things that happened to the poor animals on the site in years past. Just like human pain, the pain of animals can fill a location.

At that moment, Dave reported a burning sensation on his neck. When we checked on him, we saw a fresh scratch mark that ran from his neck all the way to his chin. As he stood there, Dave reported another burning sensation, this one on his face. Again, a scratch appeared on the side of his face. This was going to be an active place!

We quickly set up the equipment and started a session with the spirit box. A number of eerie responses came forth including the voices of little children. In fact, before we even asked any questions, the voice of a little boy came through the box saying: *"help me."*

I proceeded to try to talk to the child that seemed to be present. Every time I would ask the boy a question, a different voice would answer. This one was deep and gravelly and seemed to be stopping the young boy from speaking. The voice was making nasty comments and references to demonic names.

I decided to recite some prayers which just seemed to agitate the deep voice all the more, causing it to continue dominating the ghost box.

Something kept nagging at me intuitively, something related to my Saint Michael necklace.

Sitting on the corner of a couch in the room, I asked:

"Is my pendant being mentioned to me because of an attempt to attack or scratch me?"

At this moment, a rem pod we had placed on the stairway outside the room was going off. Phil, who was over near the device, reported a strange sensation on his back, what he described as a strong pinch. He lifted his jacket and Dave and I saw a scratch on his back. We put a light on the area to see it better, and, as we watched, another scratch formed going in the other direction.

We stood there in amazement as an upside down cross appeared on Phil. We treated the scratches with holy water and told Phil to take it easy for a moment.

It was a creepy event considering we were in a location once used for worship and religious practice. Was something trying to mock what was once a holy site?

We continued our investigation upstairs. Over and over during this investigation, the sounds of children came through various devices. I found myself very disturbed at the implication that the spirits of children could be trapped here. No souls should have to suffer being trapped in some lost state, especially the souls of children.

Every time I attempted to talk to the child voices coming over the spirit box, the deep nasty voice would return and prevent them from answering me, speaking over top of them and drowning out their voices.

One of the few times we clearly head a child's voice, it stated:

"The priest did this."

The deep voice came in again and responded:

"I enjoyed it and have no remorse."

I started reciting the Hail Mary and after a moment, I

switched to the Archangel Saint Michael protection prayer. I said several prayers asking that any children stuck at the location be free to go to God.

When I was finished, we tried to get more responses from the spirit box. For almost twenty minutes, nothing at all came through. Finally, I asked, "Did these prayers help?"

In response came a voice that said, *"they are free."*

I had hoped my faith and my prayers had helped at least some spirits that were still at the Rectory. If the response on the spirit box was true, then it was confirmation of that.

We closed down and packed up the equipment, it was time for all of us to head home.

Two nights later, lying in my own bed falling asleep, I heard a screaming voice in my ear saying, *"the children, the children."*

The voice was angry and violent and issued threats saying, *"you son of a bitch, I will slit your throat!"*

The voice continued its mantra of *"the children, the children"* over and over with obvious anger. I rose and grabbed the holy water and blessed salt and covered my room while saying protection prayers. As I did so, the voice faded away. Since I had helped the spirits of the children at the Rectory, I had angered something and now it wanted to attack me.

While I had to keep my guard up and continue a regular course of protection prayers, I also felt a sense of accomplishment at the idea that I had helped the spirits of children find some peace.

CHAPTER EIGHTEEN:
A Familiar Spirit

Since I still needed to pay some bills while I was pursuing music, I took up a job at a medical credit card company. There were a lot of other employees and one of the people I became friends with was a guy named Will. Will sat next to me in the office and he often overhead my stories and conversations about the paranormal.

One day, Will opened up and started telling me about experiences he and his girlfriend Billie were having in their apartment. He woke one night to see a shadow figure come out of his mirror and move to his side of the bed.

Will also told me that a framed picture of himself as a child was knocked over on to the floor and shattered. He was adamant that the picture wasn't knocked over by any natural means. It was on a dresser in the guest room and no one was staying in the room at the time. There were no windows open to create a draft and no vibrations that could have moved the photo from its spot.

The same night the picture was found shattered, Will had a disturbing dream. He dreamed that a man was hanging from a rope in the window of his room. The man was staring at him. The man came into the house and jumped into the mirror.

Billie had reported creepy noises in the apartment and she

too felt as if there was something paranormal going on. I offered to come by one night and see if I could find any evidence for them.

At the apartment, we all sat and talked for a while about the incidents they had experienced. I didn't sense anything negative in the place, but it did feel as if there was a presence there.

I started running an SLS camera, a device that maps anomalies and maps them as stick figures when they manifest. Will and Billie were sitting on the couch together and I aimed the camera at them. As I watched, a stick figured was mapped behind them. It kept appearing and then disappearing, but always right behind where they were sitting.

We moved into the bedroom and stood by the mirror that Will had dreamed about seeing a man jump into.

Will wanted to know if the presence in the apartment was that of his brother Manny. I turned on an SB7 spirit box and asked if Manny was there. *"Yes,"* came the reply.

Things suddenly made sense to Will. His brother Manny had gone down a dark path many years previously.

"My brother passed in 1992 when I was eight years old, and I hadn't seen him since I was six years old because I was terrified of him. The strange thing, too, that picture that was knocked over was taken around the last time I saw him."

Will had recently gained possession of Manny's ashes. I believe in part, that is what sparked the activity in Will and Billie's apartment.

Using the SLS again, I called out to Manny and asked him to manifest in front of Will. As confirmation, a stick figure appeared on the camera right in front of Will.

I started saying prayers for Manny and Will was overcome with a wave of emotion. As Will relates:

"I finally got the opportunity to tell Manny that I love and appreciate him and let him know that I was too young to understand that he was my big brother who loved me too. I wasn't afraid of him and I know he knows that now. I was very emotional and couldn't talk anymore with tears coming down.

"Sean asked Manny if he was afraid to go into the light and that he should cross over to the other side to join our mother. Manny said yes through the spirit box. That's when Sean said a prayer to free that fear within Manny's soul. Once the prayer ended, we could no longer feel a presence amongst us. All the activity leading up to that evening was my brother reaching out for help from the spiritual realm and I believe we were able to give him just that."

With David Weatherly at Revenant Acres.
(photo courtesy David Weatherly)

CHAPTER NINETEEN:
Halloween 2016

It was Halloween week of 2016 and I was ready for another road trip to hit some haunted locations. This time, I would be out with two veteran investigators, my friend Dave Spinks, and David Weatherly. Both men have been in the field for many years and I was excited to be included in their investigations. It's always great to be out with others who are passionate about the paranormal and have a lot of knowledge to share.

Our first stop was an old farmhouse in Charlottesville, Indiana called "Revenant Acres." The old house is as creepy as something from a horror movie and little is known about its history. According to local law enforcement, the place was used as a drug house for a time, an odd thing considering that it sits off on its own with a large field around it.

David and Dave had investigated the location before and they had really talked it up. While they didn't give away too many details, they did state it was one of the nastiest places they had done. That was saying a lot coming from these two guys.

On their previous investigation, David had been bitten on the leg by something unseen. It left teeth impressions and was in the shape of a human mouth. The bite appeared through a thick pair of jeans. When I saw the photo of the bite, it was shocking.

I started to wonder exactly what we were getting into.

We arrived at the location early, so I could see the outside and snap a few photos. Since we had some time to burn, we headed to the nearest town and grabbed something to eat. After eating, we walked around and took in some of the local history.

Sitting in a local coffee shop, we discussed the upcoming investigation. David and Dave showed me a video from another investigative team. In the video, a young man appears to become possessed. He leaned in close to a man several times his size and began to speak in a "layered voice." You could hear a voice coming from his mouth, but behind it, you could hear another voice. Drooling and contorting himself, he stated *"I am seven."*

The video was very disturbing.

I had posted some photos of the house online and a friend of mine saw them and contacted me right away. Judy is a psychic who has proven her skills to me on many occasions, so I was anxious to hear what she had to say about the old farmhouse. Without having any information about the location, Judy told me she felt the spirit of an angry woman was inside the house.

"She will lash out at any men who come inside" Judy told me. She went on to explain that the woman had been tortured and raped in the house before she was finally murdered there.

"That woman is consumed with evil now."

Was this woman the spirit that bit David on a previous investigation? I was now both excited and a little nervous to start our investigation.

The house is not very large. There are two floors, a few rooms on the first floor and only one room on the second floor.

A kitchen sits at the back of the house and overlooks the back yard. The kitchen would be our command center where all the equipment was kept. We were also live streaming the event on YouTube, so things could be monitored from this main spot.

There's a piano in the main living room and this is the spot where a lot of activity has been recorded by various teams. It's also the spot where David was bitten. We started out that night by the piano and turned on a ghost box. Right away, all of our names came over the box, something was well aware of our presence.

Dave Spinks was sitting on the piano bench and holding the ghost box. After a flurry of negative responses and statements out of the box, he said he felt something draining his energy.

A smell flooded through the room that was so foul, the only thing it could be compared to is human excrement and rotting flesh.

Spinks said he needed to take a break and handed me the ghost box. He walked away so he could shake off whatever was trying to influence him.

As soon as the box was in my hands, another string of threats and nasty comments came out. "Death, demon, kill you, kill you."

I started reciting prayers of protection. When I was finished, I asked out loud:

"Was a woman tortured, raped and killed here?"

"*Yes*" said a female voice.

After this, there was a string of words relating to drugs, violence and death.

At this point David and I were standing in the middle of the living room. The floor started shaking. We tried everything we could to find an explanation for the shaking, but there was nothing, no way to debunk it.

David now sat down on the piano bench and held the spirit box. Again, a long string of negative responses came out. David started asking if the spirits remembered him from his last visit. There were more negative responses and threats. Then he asked who had bitten him before. A strange female voice laughed over the ghost box.

After a couple of more questions, I noticed David was starting to look funny, like he was shaking something off. He said his ears were ringing and something was trying to push on him to influence him. David has a shamanic background and his own layers of protection, and he told me he needed to step away for a moment to ensure he had it all cleared.

He stood up and placed the spirit box on top of the piano. Just as he had let it go, a voice yelled out over the spirit box—it was my voice!

I'm blessed with ears that are very attuned to sounds, it's one of the things I employ a lot as a musician, and having worked in recording studios, there was no mistaking the sound of my own voice. Something was mimicking me.

This was the first time I ever experienced this, and it was stunning. Demonic entities can mimic the living and the dead, but to hear it using my voice was creepy.

David and I were both stunned at this incident and he snatched the spirit box back up off the piano and handed it to me.

"Call it out" he said.

I tried to get an answer as to what was using my voice. Again, the responses were a string of foul language and threats as well as references to demonic forces.

I worked with the spirit box a bit, but then I too started to feel the same energy trying to push into me as David had reported. I felt the force running through my hands and up to my left shoulder. Half my body became numb and I was worried I would slip into a trance. I now believed something in the house was, in turn, trying to possess each of us just as it had possessed the kid in the video.

Seeing that I was having the same reaction, the guys suggested we take a break and we shut the spirit box off.

We all stepped outside to get some air. I brought out some holy water and flung it on all of us while saying additional prayers. The guys had not been kidding about the intensity of this location!

Dave told us that when he was outside earlier, he thought he had seen something strange when looking in through the kitchen window. He asked me to stand inside as a point of reference, while he stood in his original position and took some photos.

He snapped about ten pics, and in only one of them, a weird figure appeared. It looked like a man with a disfigured face and large goat horns.

We stood in the kitchen looking at the pics again and again. The image of the horned creature was so disturbing, I took the holy water back out and dowsed us all again. As I was doing so, I caught something moving in my peripheral vision.

It all happened in a flash. I realized there was something in the doorway, staring at us. It had a pale, white face, black eyes and horrific teeth. I screamed out and the other guys started asking me what it was. The thing was gone. One second it was there, and the next it had vanished. I quickly blurted out what I saw and where.

David grabbed the closest thing to him, an Ovilus 5 and darted to the doorway right where it had been standing. The device spit out a flurry of words:

"Devil"

"Minion"

"Pray"

As this was happening, Dave Spinks had grabbed a bottle of triple blessed holy water and begin throwing it all around us, stating we were protected and the creature could not attack us.

As all of this was happening, at the same time, the unexplained foul odor returned, rolling through the house in waves. It was so intense it was nauseating.

After the odor passed, the Ovilus went quiet and it seemed still for a few minutes. It was eerie though and we all took a breath, wondering what was going to happen next.

We had decided to move part of the equipment closer to the living room and started to adjust some things around. Dave went and took his jacket off the back of a chair where it had been hanging for a couple of hours.

He reached into the jacket pocket and found a recorder he had left there. He stood looking at it and said, guys, this thing is recording!

Something had started the recorder while it was in the jacket. No one physically had been near the jacket for a long time. As it turned out, it had recorded the series of events from my sighting of the weird figure staring at us.

The recorder yielded more evidence. We listened as we heard the events unfold on the recorder, my yelling about the thing watching us, David using the Ovilus and Dave throwing the holy water around.

When David asked the Ovilus questions, we heard the answers recorded, but there was more. Another voice was also answering him, and this one was caught on the recorder. When David asked where the creature was, a voice said, *"beneath the floor."*

Another voice screamed on the recorder *"You better pray!"*

And when the holy water was being thrown about, a moaning voice states *"it burns ."*

Standing there listening to the recording, we all looked down at the floorboards. Was there something below us as the voice stated?

Just then, we noticed the rotting flesh smell moving through the house again.

We tried to gather some more evidence, but things went quiet. It wasn't a comfortable quiet though. It felt as if something was still there, gathering its strength for the next phase.

We took a break and prepared for the next part of our investigation. We would be conducting some sessions in the upstairs room.

It was after midnight when we started setting up our equipment. I looked around closely. Although I had checked it out briefly when we first arrived, I hadn't spent any significant time in the room. The whole house had a heaviness to it, but the upstairs even more so. Almost immediately I felt like something was trying to press on me again, and I said some prayers to shake it off.

The room was the location where the possession had taken place. We started a spirit box, and as usual in this location, the result was a string of foul words, threats and nasty responses to anything asked.

All of us stood in the room and tried out some different experiments to see what would happen. Not long after we were up there, we started hearing noises downstairs. Footsteps, whispering, scuffling, it was as if someone, or rather, several people were down there.

Dave pulled his flashlight out and walked over to the heating vent on the floor. It was an old-style vent and you could look through it and see all the way to the first floor. "I don't see anyone" he reported.

We called out in case someone had entered the house, but there was no reply.

A few seconds later, there was a loud boom and the entire house shook! It wasn't just the floor like we experienced earlier, this time it was as if something large had struck the house. It was so surreal, and we were all shocked.

The sound was so loud that people watching the livestream heard it. It was as if a truck had run into the house.

We all stood there and each of us started to experience vertigo. We had turned the spirit box off and were trying to figure out what just happened.

As we stood there trying to gain our senses, Dave noted the footsteps and scuffling noise downstairs was getting louder. We listened closely. David pointed out that whatever it was, it now sounded like it was coming up the steps towards us.

Along with the strange footsteps, we heard angry whispering. It would get very close, then it would fade away for a moment before starting again. Each time, it seemed it was getting a little closer.

We backed up in a defensive posture, not sure what might be coming through the door at us.

David pointed out that whatever it was, it was gaining more strength. Dave noted that it was probably best if we closed things down and finished at that point.

None of us are the types to leave investigations, but it always pays to be smart. We'd had a long night and gathered a ton of evidence. Rather than risk further attempts at something pushing on our energy fields, we closed out the livestream and ended the investigation.

It still took us some time to pack everything up and clear out, and we were careful to once again bless ourselves and even our vehicles before we put the old farmhouse in the rearview mirror.

We slept soundly that night, but the investigation was certainly one for the books.

Society of the Supernatural at Kosciusko County Jail.

CHAPTER TWENTY:

Two Nights in the Kosciusko Jail

The week of investigations had been intense, and our last stop promised to be crazy. We headed to the historic Kosciusko County Jail in Warsaw, Indiana.

It's a huge gothic revival building built in 1870. It's now owned by the County Historical Society and is a museum.

It sounded like it was going to be a great investigation, and again, Weatherly and Spinks had given me very little information about the site.

In fact, it wasn't until we were standing there looking at the imposing old building that David and Dave announced to me that we would be sleeping in the old jail the next two nights. I honestly thought they were joking at first, or that there would be some real bedrooms somewhere inside the big place. Turned out, that wasn't the case. We were to sleep in cells that once housed hardened criminals.

The location was large and there were a lot of historic items. We were given a tour of the main areas and some of the highlights were pointed out, but there was so much it was hard to keep up.

The first night, we had a lot of activity. Strange noises, disembodied voices and more. We investigated one cell that was reputed to have held a child molester. A lot of devices were going off in there including a rem pod.

I didn't personally like the feeling in that cell at all. I stood in there by myself and addressed the spirit of the criminal who had spent so much time in there.

"Do you feel guilty for what you did? You were found guilty; do you feel any regret for your crimes?"

I felt a presence behind me. It was as real as if a physical person were standing there. I turned around quickly and saw, in the corner of the cell, a ball of orange energy the size of a grapefruit, floating. It became brighter for a moment, then disappeared.

We had a range of other incidents that night, including a large piece of metal being knocked off a table.

As we wrapped up our first night, I had to face the fact I was sleeping in a creepy jail cell. Not only that, but the one David and Dave left me was on the main floor, right across from the molester's cell.

The jail was two stories, and the other guys would be sleeping upstairs, leaving me on the main floor by myself. Going into my cell, I noted there were two bunks. I had a cell mate—a mannequin dressed up like a prisoner. Could the night get any creepier?

The metal bed was terribly uncomfortable, and I had to keep my guard up, not knowing what kind of entities may try to screw with me while I was sleeping. I said my protection prayers, threw some holy water around and blessed things, then tried to settle in.

It was a rough night. Throughout the night and into the early morning hours, I kept hearing noises and my sleep was constantly interrupted. Whispered voices, movements, and a lot of mumbling. I was able to catch words here and there, including references to the pedophile across the room from me.

Other times I would suddenly hear the slamming of jail cell doors, or the banging of metal as something clanged against cell bars. This was not a peaceful location.

The next night we spent some time investigating a solitary confinement cell on the second floor. We all had experiences and relevant responses from various pieces of equipment.

It's important to note here that Dave Spinks is a retired law enforcement officer who spent time working for the Department of Corrections. Because of that, his presence in haunted jails always elicits a good number of responses.

During one of our periods of down time that evening, David discovered a back stairway near the kitchen. As it turned out, there were two more floors to explore. The area took up a large portion of the building and David learned it was the old residence area where the County Sheriff and his family would have lived. It was a treasure trove, filled with historical antiques and furnishings. There were numerous display cases filled with things related not just to the jail, but to the county, too. An area with railroad items, another with musical instruments, medical equipment, and even an area filled with creepy dolls.

The area was fascinating, so we decided to move our investigation and see what we could find around all the historic items.

The doll area was an obvious choice and we received several strange responses. At one point, David was using a spirit box at the end of the hallway. Behind him was a door with a small window in it. During the session, Spinks spotted a weird face peering in the window behind Weatherly. He pointed it out right away and asked what the heck it was.

Weatherly immediately took the few steps back to the door and looked in. Seeing nothing, he shone his flashlight in the small window. It turned out the door was actually an opening for an elevator, but there was nothing behind the window, only the darkness of an empty elevator shaft. The elevator itself was resting at the bottom floor of the museum.

A flurry of responses started coming over the spirit box and we turned on the SLS camera to see what else we could pick up. At this end of the hallway, there was a large, glass display case full of antique medical equipment.

We also had an Ovilus running and it too was picking up

relevant words to the events that started to unfold.

The SLS picked up a figure near David that was trying to hit him. He swung back at it to see if there was a reaction, and the figure fell back.

Dave took a turn at the same spot, and the stick figure manifested again, this time it was ready to fight and started kicking its legs at Dave and shaking one of its arms as if it was giving him the finger.

We traded off and I stood in front of the cabinet of medical equipment with a spirit box running. I felt a strange sensation and the guys reported that the stick figure had returned. Now, it was on top of the cabinet and suddenly, as Dave and David watched on the SLS camera, the figure wrapped its legs around me, as if trying to hold me still, while it started poking something into my head.

David yelled, "It's trying to give you a lobotomy!"

It was a crazy end to the investigation that night. Once we closed down our live stream, and did some more work, it was the early hours of the morning. There was little sleep again that night and the bangs, slamming cell doors and endless chatter continued through the night.

The next day we packed up all our gear and started off on the long journey home. After two restless nights in jail, I was looking forward to my own comfortable bed back home in New York.

Photo by *Gabriel Matula on Unsplash*

CHAPTER TWENTY-ONE:
Back to New York

I had left my car at Phil's apartment while I was on my Halloween trip, so when I landed back in NY, I stopped in to see him and fill him in on some of the crazy things that had happened. I was still on an energy high from all of the experiences, but at the same time, I was exhausted in every way I could imagine.

Back at home, finally in the comfort of my own bed, I quickly dozed off. Right away, I was experiencing a series of weird visions. The angry face of a woman filled with rage and holding a knife. Phil was in the vision, and the woman started stabbing him to death. When she had killed Phil, she turned her attention on me and I began to pray.

I woke from the dream, blessed my room with holy water and went back to sleep. I later shared the dream with Phil and he reported that he'd also had a dream of a woman trying to stab him.

My guard is always up. There are always things waiting to break through a crack in your aura, waiting to cause chaos in your life or to take revenge for vendettas they hold against you for doing God's work.

For me, trying to help spirits in need is the same as trying to help an injured person on the side of the road, it's the human thing to do.

Life goes on beyond the physical plane. God created us to develop our potential and each day, we have to make the choice to do the right thing and to make a difference in the world, to bring light and to be a positive force. It's not always easy to do, but it is always rewarding. Love others the way you want to be loved and do for others things that you would want done for you. Everywhere you go, try to spread the understanding of universal love.

God leaves us all clues to help us on our paths and I embrace every moment God gives me here. Thank you for reading my book. I hope it will deliver a message for each of you and that you all find magic in everyday life.

God bless you on your individual journey and in your soul's purpose. Believe in yourself!

"Saint Michael Slaying the Devil"
Painting by Raffaello Sanzio (Raphael),1518 (public domain)

Prayers

Included below are some of the prayers I use on a regular basis for protection. I hope they will assist you in your times of need.

Prayer to Saint Michael

Holy Michael, the Archangel, defend us in battle. Be our safeguard against the wickedness and snares of the devil. May God rebuke him, we humbly pray; and do you, O Prince of the heavenly host, by the power of God, cast him into hell Satan and all the evil spirits who wander through the world seeking the ruin of souls.

Amen

Saint Patrick Breastplate

I arise today

Through a mighty strength, the invocation of the Trinity,

Through belief in the Threeness,

Through confession of the Oneness

Of the Creator of creation.

I arise today

Through the strength of Christ's birth with His baptism,

Through the strength of His crucifixion with His burial,

Through the strength of His resurrection with His ascension,

Through the strength of His descent for the judgement

of doom.

I arise today

Through the strength of the love of cherubim,

In the obedience of angels,

In the service of archangels,

In the hope of resurrection to meet with reward,

In the prayers of patriarchs,

In the predictions of prophets,

In the preaching of apostles,

In the faith of confessors,

In the innocence of holy virgins,

In the deeds of righteous men.

I arise today, through

The strength of heaven,

The light of the sun,

The radiance of the moon,

The splendor of fire,

The speed of lighting,

The swiftness of wind,

The depth of the sea,

The stability of the Earth,

The firmness of rock.

I arise today, through

God's strength to pilot me,

God's might to uphold me,

God's wisdom to guide me,

God's eye to look before me,

God's ear to hear me,

God's word to speak for me,

God's hand to guard me,

God's shield to protect me

From snares of devils,

From temptation of vices,

From everyone who shall wish me ill,

Afar and near.

I summon today

All these powers between me and those evils,

Against every cruel and merciless power

That may oppose my body and soul,

Against incantations of false prophets,

Against black laws of pagandom,

Against false laws of heretics,

Against craft of idolatry,

Against spells of witches and smiths and wizards,

Against every knowledge that corrupts man's body and soul;

Christ to shield me today

Against poison, against burning,

Against drowning, against wounding,

So that there may come to me an abundance of reward.

Christ with me,

Christ before me,

Christ behind me,

Christ in me,

Christ beneath me,

Christ above me,

Christ on my right,

Christ on my left,

Christ when I lie down,

Christ when I sit down,

Christ when I arise,

Christ in the heart of every man who thinks of me,

Christ in the mouth of everyone who speaks of me,

Christ in every eye that see me,

Christ in every ear that hears me.

I arise today

Through a mighty strength, the invocation of the Trinity,

Through belief in the Threeness,

Through confession of the Oneness

Of the Creator of creation.

Prayer For Protection Against Demons
(Saint John Bosco, 1880)

O Mary, powerful Virgin,

You are the mighty and glorious Protector of the Church.

You are the Marvelous Help of Christians.

You are Terrible as an Army set in Battle Array.

You alone have destroyed every heresy in the entire Church.

In the midst of my anguish, my struggles and my distress,

Defend me from the power of the enemy,

And at the hour of my death,

Receive my soul into Paradise.

Novena to Saint Benedict

Glorious Saint Benedict, sublime model of virtue, pure vessel of God's grace!

Behold me humbly kneeling at your feet.

I implore you in your loving kindness to pray for me before the throne of God.

To you I have recourse in the dangers that daily surround me.

Shield me against my selfishness and my indifference to God and to my neighbor.

Inspire me to imitate you in all things.

May your blessing be with me always, so that I may see and serve Christ in others and work for His Kingdom.

Graciously obtain for me from God those favors and graces which I need so much in the trials, miseries and afflictions of life.

Your heart was always full of love, compassion and mercy toward those who were afflicted or troubled in any way.

You never dismissed without consolation and assistance anyone who had recourse to you.

I therefore invoke your powerful intercession, confident in the hope that you will hear my prayers and obtain for me the special grace and favor I earnestly implore.

(mention your prayer)

Help me, great Saint Benedict, to live and die as a faithful child of God, to run in the sweetness of His loving will, and to attain the eternal happiness.

"Shapeshifter" CD

For me, music is emotional, powerful and spiritual. Over time, my personal style of music has evolved and has been strongly influenced by my time investigating the paranormal. Included below are the lyrics to the songs from my latest CD release, "Shapeshifter."

"Shapeshifter"

Lie and wait for the dawn to break

through my eyes I've seen darkness awake

reaching hints of hope to bring me
the garden of peace painted on every shadow's reach
can't you feel the fight within?
surrounded in a city of ruin
a heart that needs a special pulse to
live in the light when it spreads
love that screams only to share

Here we stand to face all enemies
shape-shifting hurdles to seize
even in our own reflection
there is a win with every chance we take

The lies and guilt that stir up storms
plastered on the walls of refuge is worn
looking up from this bottomless pit
I can still feel the light transmit
encouraging messages of grace

Here we stand to face all enemies
shape-shifting hurdles to seize
even in our own reflection
there is a win with every chance we take

"How I want You So Bad"

Never thought I would see it
the end of this deep inner search

like a picture taken in my mind
as if i was already with you in a lovely blur

giving light on what never gives way
is what lead me here to say

How I want you so bad
and I don't want to lose these new memories
will you take it all and live in the surreal
how I want you so bad

At the altar of adoring truths
you stand like a statue of virtue

you make anyone believe
in the unreachable love's imagination

giving light on what never gives way
is what lead me here to say

How I want you so bad
and I don't want to lose these new memories
will you take it all and live in the surreal
how I want you so bad

The stance I gazed upon
from this sky's view that
changed me forever

though I still seek to find
what I've not yet learned
watch this unfold with me
somewhere we've both never seen

How I want you so bad
and I don't want to lose these new memories
will you take it all and live in the surreal
how I want you so bad
and I don't want to lose with all this that can be
how I want you so bad

"That's Enough"

The light I somehow thought you always were
It was once for real but now it's fiction and fuel for me

A wave goodbye is like saying hello
When you give and say what you don't mean

It's breaking all that you ever made
What you keep inside isn't what the truth speaks with
all your silence ... no

That's enough babe what's killing me now will no more
be a weight on my shoulder

That's enough babe what's killing me now will no more
taking all that won't be yours

The lies and deceit that hid behind your eyes
Played for all the wrong reasons when it turned on me

When you give and say what you don't mean
It's breaking all that you ever made

What you keep inside isn't what the truth speaks with
all your silence ... no
That's enough babe what's killing me now will no more
be a weight on my shoulder

That's enough babe what's killing me now will no more
taking all that won't be yours

You've given me nothing
given me nothing … given me nothing

With your everything
given me nothing

That's enough babe what's killing me now will no more
be a weight on my shoulder

That's enough babe what's killing me now will no more
taking all that won't be yours
You've given me nothing
given me nothing … given me nothing

With your everything
given me nothing … given me nothing

With your everything

"Deeper Than Skin"

journey is the walk of life
the strings that pull beyond the veil
reminders to a familiar sense
the wave that takes over when our faces meet…

I can't deny what's the shining truth
like flames of the same burst
cause what I feel is deeper than skin

purpose fills the void within
the remains of the unseen flourish
with just one touch
reasons crowd my space with questions
what's the meaning I've been lead to so simply?

I can't deny what's the shining truth
like flames of the same burst
cause what I feel is deeper than skin

bound to the fate that we seek...
holding close to what I guess we'll see

I can't deny what's the shining truth
like flames of the same burst
cause what I feel is deeper than skin
I can't deny what my soul screams of
destined to confuse
cause what I feel is deeper than skin

About the Authors

Sean Austin

Feeling a spiritual connection to music from an early age, Sean started playing music and taught himself several instruments by the time he was a teenager. He has written and recorded original music and performed as an opening act for numerous bands around the country.

Sean's music has been called "emotional and genuine" in the vein of Pearl Jam and the Goo Goo Dolls.

His acclaimed CD, "Shapeshifter" was released in 2017.

When a series of strange experiences led him to delve into the world of the paranormal, he found his second passion— exploring the unknown and the afterlife.

A lifelong Catholic, Sean believes his faith and religious views are a key component in his pursuit to understand the world beyond and to communicate with spirits. His time in the paranormal helped open latent psychic abilities that he continues to explore and develop.

Sean Austin was also a cast member on Destination America's three-episode show, "Demon Files" where he worked with well-known demonologist Ralph Sarchie.

Between music gigs, he continues to explore haunted locations around the country.

Find Sean online at his periscope channel and on YouTube:

https://www.pscp.tv/seandaustin

Youtube.com/seanaustinsmusic

Twitter.com/seandaustin

David Weatherly

David Weatherly is a renaissance man of the strange and supernatural. He has traveled the world in pursuit of ghosts, cryptids, UFOs, magic and more. From the specters of dusty castles, to remote, haunted islands, from ancient sites, to modern mysteries, he has journeyed to the most unusual places on the globe seeking the unknown.

David became fascinated with the paranormal at a young age. Ghost stories and accounts of weird creatures and UFOs led him to discover many of his early influences. Writers such as such as John Keel, Jacques Vallee, Hans Holzer and others set him on course to spend his life exploring and investigating the unexplained.

Throughout his life, he's also delved into shamanic and magical traditions from around the world, spending time with elders from numerous cultures in Europe, the Americas, Africa and Asia. He has studied with Taoist masters in China, Tibetan Lamas, and other mystics from the far east. He's picked up knowledge from African and Native American tribal elders and sat around fires with shaman from countless other traditions.

Along his path, David has also gathered a lot of arcane knowledge, studying a range of ancient arts from palmistry, the runes, and other obscure forms of divination to alchemy and magick. He has studied and taught Qigong and Ninjutsu as well as various energy related arts. David has also studied stage and performance magic.

His shamanic and magical background has given him a unique perspective in his explorations into the unknown, and he continues to write, travel and explore, leaving no stone unturned in his quest for the strange and unusual.

David has investigated, and written about, a diverse range of topics including, Hauntings, Cryptozoology, Ufology, Ancient Mysteries, Shamanism, Magic and Psychic Phenomena.

In 2012, David founded the independent media and publishing company, Leprechaun Productions.

He has been a featured speaker at conferences around the world and has lectured for countless paranormal, UFO, and spiritual groups.

He is a frequent guest on Coast to Coast AM with George Noory, Darkness Radio and other radio programs. David has also appeared on numerous television shows including Ancient Aliens, Mysteries at the National Parks and Beyond Belief.

David's books include Strange Intruders, Black Eyed Children and the Wood Knocks and Haunted series.

To find David online:

http://twocrowsparanormal.blogspot.com/

Made in the USA
Columbia, SC
06 July 2018